Gregory Wolfe's vision is the animating force behind *Image,* one of the best journals on the planet. *Intruding Upon the Timeless,* a collection of his pieces from *Image,* takes its title from a phrase of Flannery O'Connor. That's apt, because not since O'Connor's *Mystery and Manners* has there been such bracing insight on the pile-up where art and faith collide. This book will rev your engines and propel you down the same road.

—**Annie Dillard,** Pulitzer Prize-winning author of
Pilgrim at Tinker Creek

Gregory Wolfe's reflections from his editor's chair are much more: they are spiritual essays. For, with a prose as fine and sharp as a surgeon's knife, Wolfe manages, over and over, to cut very close to the soul.

—**Richard Rodriguez,** author of *Hunger of Memory*
and *Days of Obligation*

In an age that has been facilely identified as secularized or post-Christian, Gregory Wolfe was among the first to perceive instead a renaissance of religious humanism in the arts: of writers and artists who did not abandon their faith in Mystery but drew courage, guidance, and inspiration from it. The trenchant and erudite short essays of *Intruding Upon the Timeless* serve as a stirring introduction to that popular but rather subterranean movement, and establish Gregory Wolfe as one of the most incisive and persuasive voices of our generation.

—**Ron Hansen,** author of *Mariette in Ecstasy* and *Atticus*

For nearly two decades, Gregory Wolfe has kept a keen eye on the increasingly busy crossroads of art and religion in America; his initiating and ongoing insight has led to a wealth of significant accomplishment, but the most sustained (on his part) and sustaining (in the service of countless others) has been his shepherding of *Image: A Journal of the Arts and Religion.* While these editorial essays can serve, most readily, as documents of recent literary and art history, recording the surprising renewal of substantive religious thought in both, we would do well to bear in mind that each has served, in its turn, as initiating, encouraging, visionary impulse for much of what it both describes and brings into being.

—**Scott Cairns,** author of *Philokalia: New and Selected Poems*

Square Halo
is quickly
becoming
a leader
in the
realm of
Christianity
and the arts

—Image: A Journal of the Arts & Religion

It Was Good: Making Art to the Glory of God is a collection of thirteen essays covering a wide range of topics focussed on the practice of making art from a Christian worldview. "We recommend *It Was Good: Making Art to the Glory of God* to you. It will help you think Christianly about art, stimulate you to be creative for God's glory, introduce you to some artists who are seeking to glorify God in their work, and … cause you to stop and worship the One whose glory is beautiful beyond all imagining." —CRITIQUE

"*Objects of Grace: Conversations on Creativity and Faith* is a colorful and concise collection of interviews and art from some of America's most intriguing Christian artists … Sandra Bowden, Dan Callis, Mary McCleary, John Silvis, Edward Knippers, Erica Downer, Albert Pedulla, Tim Rollins, Joel Sheesley, and Makoto Fujimura. This group gives a vivid account of what it means for God's grace to be incarnated into the visual arts in our postmodern world … The sheer beauty of the design and production values of this book is itself a major achievement, one that gives hope both for the church and the larger culture." —IMAGE

Light at Ground Zero: St. Paul's Chapel After 9/11 is a picture essay telling of the relief work carried on at St. Paul's Chapel, an 18th-century Episcopal church that stands less than one hundred yards from the World Trade Center site. Accented with fragments of prayers and Scripture, these photographs show the love, encouragement and radical hospitality offered to the men and women who labored after September 11 in the most difficult and challenging context anyone ever could have imagined.

Intruding Upon the Timeless
Meditations on Art, Faith, and Mystery

Gregory Wolfe
Engravings by Barry Moser

Intruding Upon the Timeless
Meditations on Art, Faith, and Mystery

Gregory Wolfe
Engravings by Barry Moser

Square Halo Books

First Edition 2003
Copyright ©2003 Square Halo Books
P.O. Box 18954, Baltimore, MD 21206
www.SquareHaloBooks.com

ISBN 0-9658798-5-2
Library of Congress Control Number: 2003105194

Printed in the Unites States of America

For Suzanne, Magdalen, Helena,
Charles, and Benedict

Contents

Engravings

Preface

FOR much of the twentieth century, there was at least one issue on which the vast majority of both religious believers and the secular intellectuals agreed: that great art inspired by a profound grappling with the Judeo-Christian faith was a thing of the past. That there were a few exceptions, such as T.S. Eliot and a handful of other writers, only seemed to prove the rule.

The pious had become estranged from modern culture, reacting to the secularization of the modern era with fear, and withdrawing into their own increasingly isolated subcultures. Ironically, as those religious subcultures pulled away from the realm of literature and high art, they began to ape the forms of popular culture—merely substituting edifying religious clichés for the marketplace idols of sex, money, and power.

At the same time, the gatekeepers of high culture, following Freud, treated religion as escapism. To the extent that faith was an

exercise in wish-fulfillment, it stood as the antithesis of art's obligation to confront and penetrate reality. Thus the appearance of
religious themes, experiences, or symbols in a work of art could only
bring about a short-circuiting of the drama and persuasiveness of
that work.

Though it ruled for most of the century, this strange consensus
among intellectuals and believers began to break down toward the
end. The secular master narratives, such as Marxism and
Freudianism, had failed to live up to their initial promise; instead of
bringing the light of scientific reason to human affairs, they left their
adherents unable to account for the true wellsprings of good and evil.
And among the faithful there was a growing number who felt that
cultural isolation had reduced religion to rationalism and legalism.

The breakdown of that consensus led to an equally odd conver-
gence: a hunger, on the part of both secularist and believer, for a
deeper understanding of mystery, that borderland where reason fails
and only faith and imagination can go. These two faculties reach out
beyond rigid and divisive ideological categories into paradox and
ambiguity. In the end, the mystery of mysteries may be that only in
paradox and ambiguity can truth be glimpsed.

It was at this moment of cultural and religious change that
Image: A Journal of the Arts and Religion was born. Those of us
involved in its founding were only dimly aware of those larger forces
of change. Indeed, there was a great deal of self-questioning among
us, not only about whether a literary and arts quarterly could be
financially sustainable, but as to whether the work we hoped was
being created was actually being created. Would we find material to
fill more than three or four issues?

We needn't have worried. What we discovered was that our interest in the intersection between faith and imagination was shared by myriad artists and writers all over the world. The goal then became how to present this creative resurgence on the part of artists grappling with religious faith to both the church and mainstream culture. The first principle had to be aesthetic excellence: what we published had to be good art, able to stand alongside the best that was being produced. It followed that *Image* had to be present on the public square, and not in some sort of self-imposed religious ghetto. For it is precisely in the imaginative space created by works of art that a diverse, multicultural society can explore religious matters without the divisiveness of polemics and propositions. Finally, we believed that the range of material we presented had to come from both those whose religious faith was more settled and those who were struggling with doubt and dissent. The interaction of these two groups helps keep each honest and open.

In a time dominated by political and ideological contention, *Image* gives primacy to the creative voice. The majority of its pages are filled with fiction, poetry, creative nonfiction, and critical expositions of visual art, music, dance, and architecture. However, our habit has been to publish a brief editorial statement at the beginning of each issue. To be sure, it is difficult to generate sustained arguments in only one or two thousand words. But even here there has been a purpose: to keep the stress on meditation and reflection, to provoke thought rather than to exhaust it. Perhaps an analogy can be found in fiction where the tradition of the "short short" story provides readers with the prose version of haiku—the brief impression that opens up a space for further thought.

The editorials are printed in chronological order, rather than being grouped by theme or other contrivance. So they unfold as the journal (and its editor) moved through time. That there are a few repetitions in this book I hope the reader will forgive. My hope is that when they occur they will occasionally chime, sounding with a bit of resonance rather than merely falling flat. All errors of fact and judgment are entirely my own.

The meditations collected in this book are attempts to probe the ways that art and faith, poetry and prayer, can nourish and sustain one another. Too often these parallel enterprises have been collapsed into a single entity, with disastrous results. Despite the positive changes that have taken place in our society, we continue to live in an ideologically polarized world, where vacuous liberalism and rigid fundamentalism dominate public discourse. Into this fragmented and contentious world, art that engages faith can body forth an incarnational balance between the letter and the spirit, make ancient truths new, and allow the time-bound to briefly and tentatively intrude upon the timeless.

Seattle, May 31, 2003
Feast of the Visitation

Intruding Upon the Timeless

St. Thomas called art "reason in making." This is a very cold and very beautiful definition, and if it is unpopular today, this is because reason has lost ground among us. As grace and nature have been separated, so imagination and reason have been separated, and this always means an end to art. The artist uses his reason to discover an answering reason in everything he sees. For him, to be reasonable is to find, in the object, in the situation, in the sequence, the spirit which makes it itself. This is not an easy or simple thing to do. It is to intrude upon the timeless, and that is only done by the violence of a single-minded respect for the truth. —Flannery O'Connor

THE individuals who founded *Image* in the late 1980s represented a growing number of artists and theologians who had come to believe that the lack of a journal of the arts and religion constituted a serious gap in the cultural life of the West.

That gap might be described by pointing out one of the choicer ironies of modern history: the twentieth century, the era of the death of God and the rise of the great secular "master narratives," nevertheless witnessed an outpouring of art inspired by faith—a resurgence that continues into the new millennium.

But for most of the modern era, the gatekeepers of public culture embraced the belief that God was dead, or at least inaccessible. This led to a disdain for any work of art that might attempt to render the presence of grace. As Dan Wakefield wrote in a 1989 essay in the *New York Times* ("And Now, a Word From Our Creator"), many of his generation "thought that the issue of God had been settled" by F. Scott Fitzgerald, who declared, "'all wars fought, all Gods dead.'" In that influential essay, Wakefield confessed both to the poverty of his earlier prejudices and to his delight in discovering the vital tradition of art inspired by faith.

There is, however, evidence that our cultural institutions are now more open to the numinous in art. In the area of fiction, for example, the Library of America edition of the complete works of Flannery O'Connor has elevated her to the status of a classic of our literature. By the late 1980s, the reviewers began to lavish praise on recent novels by John Updike, Walker Percy, Reynolds Price, J.F. Powers, and Shusaku Endo—all of whom place Christian faith at the heart of their fictive worlds.

A culture is governed by its reigning myths. There is an increasing sense these days that materialism, whether of the Left or Right, cannot sustain or nourish our common life. Religion and art share the capacity to help us renew our awareness of the ultimate questions: who we are, where we have come from, and where we are going. In their highest forms, religion and art unite faith and reason, grace and nature; they preserve us from the twin errors of superstition and rationalist abstraction.

But religion and art also need each other. Yet another irony of the modern world has been the persistent estrangement between organized religion and the art world. In the last twenty years this estrangement gave way to its opposite: an indiscriminate use of anything that seemed modern. Perhaps we are now in a better position to achieve proper balance. When we lack the kind of attention which only the imagination can provide, we make it more difficult to live the life of faith. And art, when it sees no creation to celebrate and no soul in need of saving, loses its respect for truth.

As the examples from contemporary fiction cited above should indicate, there is no shortage of original work of the highest quality reflecting the intersection of faith and art. This is true of all the arts. *Image* exists not only to feature this creative work, but also to foster critical discourse in the areas of aesthetics and hermeneutics. Unlike some of the journals in recent decades which have been more or less exclusively interested in liturgical art, *Image* focuses on high art that is not directly in the service of worship. Nor does this journal have any interest in featuring art that is merely didactic or propagandistic; along with Keats, we "hate poetry [or any art form] that has a palpable design upon us."

Although the journal emerges out of a Christian sensibility, *Image* strives to avoid the dangers of narrow ethnocentrism or denominationalism. The journal is not, and will never be, identified with any particular school of art or aesthetic program. Moreover, the entire range of creative expression is represented in its pages: fiction, poetry, creative nonfiction, painting, sculpture, architecture, music, film, and dance.

To be sure, *Image* is an ambitious project. But nothing short of the "violence" of this commitment will be able to sustain the necessary but daunting task of intruding upon the timeless.

(*From the pilot issue, published in 1989. Written with the assistance of Harold Fickett.*)

Convergences

WHEN the pilot issue of *Image* was published in 1989, the editors knew that they had undertaken a quixotic task. The "culture wars" were then at their height. The relationship between art and religion was front page news—but only because Senator Jesse Helms and the Rev. Donald Wildmon were trading charges and counter-charges with the supporters of the National Endowment for the Arts. Irate citizens were marching for and against Andres Serrano's *Piss Christ* and Martin Scorsese's *The Last Temptation of Christ*. In this cultural High Noon, it often seemed that the fastest press conferences and largest mailing lists would determine who was left standing at the end of the day.

In short, one might question the timing of *Image's* debut.

Nonetheless, we dared to believe that we had conceived and produced a journal whose time had come. In our first editorial statement we spoke of the increasing number of artists embodying

religious experience and themes in their works. We also noted that
the cultural establishment was less monolithic in approaching the
subject of religion in art; few critics today believe that religion is
nothing more than wish-fulfillment or nostalgia.

We have been heartened by the richness and the diversity of the
poetry, fiction, visual art, memoirs, and critical essays we have
brought together in the pages of *Image*. When we stand back and
look at each issue of the journal as a whole, we find a number of
fascinating resonances between the individual contributions. Take,
for example, the two visual artists represented in our third issue. Both
Ed Knippers and Thomas Lanigan-Schmidt have turned to the
Baroque era to recover the meaning of the Incarnation—the enflesh-
ment of the divine—at a time when spirituality has become
increasingly abstract and nebulous. The memoirs of Tom Willett and
John Peters-Campbell both evoke that struggle for emotional and
spiritual maturity that has characterized many who have grown up
in the fundamentalist subculture. Another subtle resonance can be
found in the interview with Andre Dubus and the excerpt from his
son's new novel.

Sensing the relationships between the various pieces in *Image*—the
metapoetics of the journal—put us in mind of Flannery O'Connor. She
named one of her stories, and the collection in which it appeared,
"Everything That Rises Must Converge." The phrase comes from the
twentieth-century Catholic philosopher, Teilhard de Chardin. You don't
have to accept Teilhard's belief in cosmic evolution (O'Connor didn't) to
appreciate the wisdom of this saying. Whenever something is true,
good, or beautiful, whether it be art, prayer, or thought, it rises. And in
rising, it converges with everything else that is true, good, or beautiful.

O'Connor saw Teilhard's words as central to the mission of the Christian artist. For a work of art to "rise," it has to reveal that the natural world borders on the supernatural. That is the way of art: to approach mystery through indirection and metaphor.

As editors, the key question for us, when looking for material to publish in *Image,* is: Does it rise? If so, then we know that there will be important convergences arising out of each issue—convergences with the minds and hearts of our readers and convergences with the Logos, the creative principle of the universe itself.

It is difficult to maintain this editorial policy in a politicized culture, where attention spans are short, and so many people want art to fit into their own version of political or religious correctness. Judging from the enthusiastic response to the first two issues of *Image,* however, we feel that there is a growing number of people who would like to become conscientious objectors in the culture wars.

Silence, Cunning, and Exile

THE second *Image* conference was held in November 1993 in the historic town of New Harmony, Indiana. In that special place, where past and present meet—where the wooden homes of nineteenth-century religious seekers and utopians stand side by side with outstanding contemporary art and architecture—conference speakers and attendees considered the topic of "Silence, Cunning, and Exile: Saying the Unsayable in the '90s."

The conference theme was taken from a phrase out of James Joyce's autobiographical novel, *A Portrait of the Artist as a Young Man.* It is a highly suggestive phrase, one that speaks to artists in the modern era, and in particular to Christian artists. There is, however, an element of irony in using the words "silence, cunning, and exile" to address the concerns of the artist whose vision is shaped by faith. For these words signaled the young Joyce's commitment to serving the god of Art and his renunciation of his Catholic faith. Near the end of *A Portrait*, Stephen Daedalus says to his friend Cranly:

> *You have asked me what I would do and what I would not do. I*
> *will tell you what I will do and what I will not do. I will not serve*
> *that in which I no longer believe, whether it call itself my home,*
> *my fatherland, or my Church: and I will try to express myself in*
> *some mode of life or art as freely as I can and as wholly as I can,*
> *using for my defence the only arms I allow myself to use—*
> *silence, exile, and cunning.*

In this passage Joyce's *alter ego*, Daedalus, utters his *"non serviam"*—the declaration, according to tradition, that Satan made to God: "I will not serve." Joyce refuses to serve the traditional institutions—nation and religion—because they do not allow him to express his full sense of what it is to be human. Given the crisis of modern culture and the state of Irish society at the time, it is impossible not to admire Joyce for his passionate desire to speak in a new language. His act of rebellion was destined to cost him dearly, forcing him to live as an exile for the rest of his life.

The *Image* conference turned Joyce's words back on themselves. After nearly a century of Modernist experimentation in the arts, the notion of the artist as god has worn thin. Today, more and more people have come to realize that, however dramatic and powerful Joyce's rebellion was, it could only end in solipsism and despair—the last gasp of Romantic egotism. The great Christian artists of the twentieth century knew, with Joyce, that the language and institutions of Western culture had become desiccated and barren, incapable of revealing the full dimensions of our humanity. But they resorted to the stratagems of silence, cunning, and exile in order to embody their faith in a transcendent god—the God of Abraham, Isaac, and Jacob. These artists have learned that in a secular society, silence, cunning, and exile have enabled them to draw near to the mystery of faith.

One thinks, for instance, of T.S. Eliot, who, when he finally accepted the Christian faith, decided to write a poem about the birth of Christ called "Journey of the Magi." If you read that poem, you will never come across a single word that refers to Jesus, child, nativity, or Bethlehem. "A cold coming we had of it," the speaker of the poem announces in the first line. A deeply interior poem, it is a retrospective look at the psychic and spiritual effects of the Incarnation. The poem works through indirection and irony; our perspective on the Nativity is filtered through the consciousness of the dramatic *persona* of the Magus. Rather than using the exhausted, trivialized symbols of Christmas, the poem forces us to focus on the inner significance of the Incarnation.

There are, of course, many artists in the twentieth century who have pursued the same pathway. Flannery O'Connor spoke of the stratagems the Christian writer would have to use to communicate to a secular world: "to the hard of hearing you shout, and for the almost-blind you draw large and startling figures." Thus she used distortion, caricature and the grotesque to try to communicate the very same theological and spiritual points which in a past age would have comprised a common cultural heritage. In a fragmented and secularized society that is biblically illiterate, the Christian artist finds herself using guerilla tactics.

To be sure, silence, cunning, and exile are not confined to the modern era. They are metaphors for some of the perennial truths of the human condition. Though the sense of exile has been acute among many writers living in modern and postmodern society, we can refer to the Psalms of the Babylonian exile for the archetype of this experience: "How can we sing our song in a foreign land?"

Cunning is itself a fascinating word and one with a venerable ancestry. In the Bible "cunning" is used in connection with art. God's instructions for the construction of the tabernacle and temple were to be performed with cunning. Cunning has the connotation of craft—the artist's craft. It also refers to the wiliness and opportunism which the artist employs to reach his audience and communicate his deepest vision.

The most powerful of all these terms is silence. Silence is not something we experience very often today. We live in a society of noise and endless distraction. Artists have always understood and respected that the creative act emerges out of silence. Silence, of course, is a term that is appropriate for literature and music. If I had to translate the concept of silence to the visual arts, I would say that the parallels include emptiness, space, and concavity. Max Picard, a Swiss theologian of the earlier part of the century, wrote in his classic, *The World of Silence*:

Silence is a basic phenomenon. That is to say, it is a primary, objective reality, which cannot be traced back to anything else. It cannot be replaced by anything else; it cannot be exchanged with anything else. There is nothing behind it to which it can be related, except the Creator Himself.

Silence is original and self-evident like the other basic phenomena; like love and loyalty and death and life itself. But it existed before all these and is in all of them. Silence is the firstborn of the basic phenomena. It envelops other basic phenomena—love, loyalty and death; and there is more silence than speech in them, more of the invisible than the visible. There is also more silence in one person than can be used in a single human life. That is why every human utterance is surrounded by mystery. The silence in a man stretches out beyond a single human life. In this silence man is connected with past and future generations.

Out of silence emerges the creative act, both in the "sub-creation" of the artist and in the creation of God. But there is also a sense in which the created artifact itself is something sent *into* silence. Annie Dillard has spoken of fiction as a "probe" that takes soundings in the realm of mystery. In the process of writing, the novelist discovers what he or she really knows. The probe—the completed work of fiction—then returns, with "readings" that helps us to penetrate into the heart of mystery.

In the Bible, the theme of silence versus speech, of what is sayable and what is unsayable, is central. The unspeakability of God's name is a reminder that the mystery of God is not something that man can possess for himself. The God who spoke of himself as "I am who am" knows how to use indirection to speak to his audience. This theme continues in the Gospels, where the "messianic secret"—Christ's reticence about revealing his identity—requires the apostles to interpret his indirect statements, the parables.

The space that Christ gives us to respond to him is similar to the space that the artist must give to us to respond to his or her work. The artist and the mature person of faith know that we cannot simply reach into that mystery and appropriate it. The creative act is an act of reverence, an act done in humility.

The art that emerges out of silence—the art that experiences human life and our fallen world as a place of exile—forces us to ask the question "why?" All great art leads us to ask the fundamental questions: "Who am I?" "Where have I come from?" and "Where am I going?" Simone Weil, one of the most brilliant mystical writers of the twentieth century, a woman intensely Jewish and intensely Christian at the same time, spoke of suffering and beauty as the two great means by which we are forced to ask the ultimate questions:

> There can be no answer to the 'Why?' of the afflicted .... The only things that compel us to ask the question are affliction, and also beauty; for the beautiful gives us such a vivid sense of the presence of something good that we look for some purpose there, without even finding one. Like affliction, beauty compels us to ask: Why? Why is this thing beautiful? But rare are those who are capable of asking this question for as long as a few hours at a time. The afflicted man's question goes on for hours, days, years. It ceases only when he has no strength left.

He who is capable not only of crying out but also of listening will hear the answer. Silence is the answer. This is the eternal silence for which Vigny bitterly reproached God; but Vigny had no right to say how the just man should reply to this silence, for he was not one of the just. The just man loves. He who is capable not only of listening but also of loving hears this silence as the word of God.

The speech of created beings is with sounds. The word of God is silence. God's secret word of love can be nothing else but silence. Christ is the silence of God.

Why I Am a Conscientious Objector in the Culture Wars

I have a confession to make: I've burnt my draft card to the culture wars. It may sound unpatriotic and irresponsible, but I have come to the conclusion that these wars are unjust and illegitimate, and I will not fight in them. If necessary, I will move to Canada.

By now, the term "culture wars" has become part of our public vocabulary, referring to the constant political clash of opposing worldviews—call them traditionalist versus progressive or conservative versus liberal. This conflict manifests itself in a number of issues, including abortion, euthanasia, welfare, homosexual rights, the relations between church and state, and the public funding of controversial art.

My objection to the culture wars does not mean that I have no principles or refuse to stand up for them: I have strong opinions on most of these conflicts, and am willing to give voice to them when appropriate. What bothers me is the manner in which these wars are conducted.

As sociologist James Davison Hunter has pointed out in his two recent books, *Culture Wars* and *Before the Shooting Starts,* issues that are at root philosophical and theological have become utterly politicized. In other words, genuine debate and reflection on the issues has been replaced by the clash of factions fighting for absolutist, ideologically pure visions. In an interview for the Mars Hill Audio Journal, Hunter called this a conflict between "competing utopian politics that will not rest until there is a complete victory." Thus the culture wars are fought out in the political realm. Hunter concluded: "The only thing left to order public life is power. This is why we invest so much into politics."

Of course, the causes of this politicization are numerous and complex, stretching back into our spiritual and intellectual history. But the urgent need at the moment is to recognize that we cannot reduce culture and its various modes of discourse to nothing more than a political battleground. The political institutions of a society grow up out of a rich cultural life, and not the other way around. As its etymology indicates, the word culture is a metaphor for organic growth. Reducing culture to politics is like constantly spraying insecticide and never watering or fertilizing the soil.

Christians have not been immune to the pressures of living in an ideological age. They have tended to either embrace secular liberalism or react violently against it. The result is a constant movement toward one extreme or another: the Zeitgeist or the fortress mentality, trendiness or philistinism. What is needed is not some form of compromise, but a more profound sense of where the real tensions and paradoxes lie.

In his book *Christ and Culture,* H. Richard Niebuhr pointed out the limitations of seeing Christ "in culture" or "against culture." Niebuhr offered another model, the kind embraced by St. Augustine, which envisions the Christian mission as a continual engagement with, and transformation of, culture. In today's political atmosphere, the idea of transformation or conversion is seen as a highly offensive "imposition of values," but Augustine and Niebuhr were not theocrats. They believed that the life of culture ought to involve a dialectic between nature and grace, human culture and the revelation of God. Grace without nature becomes abstract and inhuman. Nature without grace tends toward despair and meaninglessness. The true paradigm is the Incarnation: Word made flesh, the human and the divine unified.

Image was founded on the premise that Christians have an obligation to nourish the culture of their time, and to enrich their faith by deepening and extending their imaginations. *Image* does not speak the language of politics but the language of art inspired by faith. That form of speech lies at the heart of our culture and it must not be allowed to become a dead language.

The format and graphic design of *Image* embody these convictions. At the risk of being called "elitist," we have chosen to feature longer stories and essays, rather than cater to short attention spans and the desire for pre-packaged polemics. We have also invested in expensive four-color reproductions in order to do justice to the visual arts. We realize that all this might convey the impression that we are "high art" snobs, but we are confident that the work in our pages is so grounded in a sense of reality that we won't be accused of separating art from life or substituting art for faith. Our hope is that

Image should, both in form and content, invite contemplation and provide aesthetic delight.

Above all, we want *Image* to play an important role in restoring a central tradition in art to the public square. Without projects like *Image,* the culture wars will continue to expand and our civic life will be increasingly politicized and tribalized. Our culture will then be like the place in Matthew Arnold's "Dover Beach," a country "where ignorant armies clash by night."

Imagination vs. Fancy

I N my earlier meditations, I have pointed out the resurgence of religious ideas and experiences in contemporary art and literature. I have argued that this phenomenon is part of an important cultural shift and a sign of hope.

But many ambiguities and ironies attend this new openness to religion, and it would be wrong to ignore them. As G.K. Chesterton reminds us, an open mind, like an open mouth, must eventually close on something nourishing, or perish. For some decades it seemed that the Judeo-Christian vision was going to be replaced by another strong, all-encompassing system, such as Marxism or Freudianism. The demise of those systems did not, however, entail a renaissance of religious orthodoxy. What we now see is a postmodern culture dominated by subjectivism and the notion that the individual creates his own set of beliefs. This has led not only to the popularity of syncretistic New Age religion, but to the spectacle of churchgoers picking and choosing among the doctrines espoused by their historic denominations.

What used to be bracing "either/or" issues of faith and conviction have now subsided into easygoing "both/and" scenarios. In popular culture, the use of religion is often little more than nostalgia, a salve to the consciences of Baby Boomers who are beginning to feel intimations of mortality. In high art this type of sentimentality is less frequent; cynicism and despair are more common. The art establishment continues to be hospitable to a number of nihilistic pranksters who desperately search for new modes of mockery and blasphemy against traditional religion.

What disturbs me, however, are the number of serious works of art that seem to bring in religious experience as a source of imagery or paradox or drama, but fail to engage that religion at the deepest levels. Take, for example, the late works by Andy Warhol that manipulate images from da Vinci's *Last Supper*. I don't doubt that Warhol's Catholicism was deeply-rooted or that these late paintings represent a struggle to renew his religious sensibility. But cropping, re-coloring, masking, and duplicating da Vinci's images do not constitute a new vision of faith. Warhol was unable to emerge from the detachment of conceptual art to a passionate engagement that placed his own life and art on the line.

Or consider the case of Brian Moore, a novelist of consummate skill. Several of Moore's recent novels focus on Catholics caught up in terrifying and complex political and moral issues. Catholicism, with its high moral demands and theology of suffering, offers Moore a dramatic framework for his protagonists. But there are times in Moore's fiction when that religious dimension seems more a source of inner psychic conflict than a sustaining force in his characters' lives.

How does one distinguish between art that merely uses religion from art that conveys a vision of the world seen through the eyes of faith? In trying to answer that question, I have found myself returning to Samuel Taylor Coleridge's famous definition of the imagination:

> *The primary imagination I hold to be the living power and prime agent of all human perception, and as a repetition in the finite mind of the eternal act of creation in the infinite I AM. The secondary I consider as an echo of the former, co-existing with the primary in the kind of its agency, and differing only in degree, and in the mode of its operation. It dissolves, diffuses, dissipates, in order to re-create; or where this process is rendered impossible, yet still, at all events, it struggles to idealize and to unify. It is essentially vital, even as all objects (as objects) are essentially fixed and dead.*
>
> *Fancy, on the contrary, has no other counters to play with but fixities and definites. The fancy is indeed no other than a mode of memory emancipated from the order of time and space; and blended with, and modified by that empirical phenomenon of the will which we express by the word choice.*

Coleridge's differentiation between the secondary, or artistic, imagination, and the fancy, goes to the heart of the matter. When religion merely functions in a work of art to enhance mood or frame a paradox it becomes a fixed and lifeless thing, a piece of cultural memory used by conscious choice, not organic and alive. However cleverly these counters are moved around, even in the hands of such talented artists as Warhol and Moore, they do not catch fire, or take us inside the experience of faith. They do not possess the seamless unity of a fully imagined work.

Does that mean that religious orthodoxy is the measure for determining the imaginative vitality of art? No. Plenty of third-rate work has come from the pens and brushes of the pious. And there are works of passionate searching, such as those of Camus, that are not produced by the dogmatically correct. But there remain the great integrated figures, from Dante and Rembrandt and Hopkins to T.S. Eliot and Rouault and Flannery O'Connor, whose integrated faith and art leave us transformed by their creations. These artists are *Image's* patron saints, precisely because their works echo the creations of the original "I AM."

The Weaker Brethren

TEN minutes (or less) into any conversation about art and religion and the subject is likely to veer toward a discussion of scandal, blasphemy, and censorship. The most common examples to be trotted out are *Piss Christ* and *The Last Temptation of Christ,* works created by artists who are rebelling against, or estranged from, the Christian faith. But there is another type of conflict under the heading of art, religion, and censorship: the conflict that occurs between Christian artists and their communities.

For those of us who believe in the importance of imagination in the life of faith, it is tempting to dismiss most of these intramural conflicts as symptomatic of Philistinism and Puritanism within the churches. We have all encountered paranoid fundamentalists looking for evidence of the occult—or for any indication whatsoever that human beings have a sexual life—in every canvas and short story they examine.

But even if we bracket off the fundamentalists and other culture warriors run amok, there are still a substantial number of thoughtful Christians who find themselves in conflict over art that is deemed too controversial to be given exposure within the community of believers. Dismissing such conflicts out of hand would not only be arrogant, but it would also deprive us of an opportunity to explore the intersection between faith and its expression through culture.

Take, for example, the recent trend among evangelicals that has brought many of them out of their cultural isolation and in quest of art that explores the entire range of human experience. Though this is one of the most heartening trends within the church, the moment of truth may have arrived: either the barriers will be breached or the signal for retreat will be sounded.

The pressure points in such conflicts center on the middlemen—the pastors, editors, music producers, and curators—who want to bring art to the larger community. Caught between cautious superiors and the possibility of rebellion from activists in their audience, these middlemen try to balance expedience and principle. They deserve sympathy and encouragement, and prayers.

When a conflict arises in this type of community, the most frequent line of reasoning put forward by those who want to restrict access to art is what I call the "weaker brethren" argument. It derives from St. Paul's discussion, in Romans 14 and 1 Corinthians 8, of actions that serve as stumbling blocks to the faith of a "weak brother." Those who are strong in their faith know that eating meats that are used for pagan rituals is acceptable; after all, meat is meat, as God well knows. But if you can avoid giving offense to the weaker brethren you should, to enable them to concentrate on more important issues.

To what extent is the weaker brethren argument applicable to the arts? The answer, it seems to me, would depend on the context. If the context is the specific locus of worship, then the argument has effect. Hanging a controversial painting behind altar or pulpit would interfere with the prayers of some of the faithful. But what of the art gallery, or the publication that is not officially tied to a church denomination? In these instances the weaker brethren argument begins to break down. The weak have responsibilities too, and the answer for them is to simply not read the book or attend the exhibition. Otherwise a small group gains absolute power over the larger community.

The problem is that those who object to allegedly controversial art do not like to think of themselves as weak. On the contrary, they claim to have a strength (i.e., orthodoxy/purity) that the permissive or liberal individuals lack. Also, it is often unclear just how these spokesmen for the weaker brethren got themselves appointed to that position. Have the brethren been scientifically polled? Is the hesitant publisher concerned about giving scandal, or only about losing sales through bad publicity or facing an unpleasant fight with his board of directors?

Presumably we have an obligation to help the weaker brethren become strong. But how is that to happen? Artists are often told that the community is "not ready" for their work, and that a gradualist approach is necessary. The problem with gradualism, however, is similar to that of an ancient Greek mathematical problem: if you travel half the distance to a point an infinite number of times, you will still never reach that point, however close you may appear to be.

There are times when experiencing the shock of the new is the only way a community can progress to a new level of insight. That has been the way with art in Western history. So long as the artists and those who mediate their work are willing to explain themselves, to provide the aesthetic and moral context of their work, there is a chance for growth. I have met very few Christian artists who take the modernist position of utter indifference to their audience. But if their work is withdrawn and left in obscurity, artists are helpless. What publishers, editors, curators, and their ilk need is courage and a demonstrable belief in the quality of the art they stand behind. Then the debate can commence. More often than not, the ranks of the weaker brethren are smaller than their spokesmen contend, and some of the brethren have been looking for the chance to grow strong.

Real Presence

THE school of literary theory known as deconstruction is now considered passé in the academy, but during its fifteen minutes of intellectual fame it encapsulated the essence of our *fin-de-siècle* malaise. The deconstructionists argued that language and art as the communication of meaning between artist and recipient was an outmoded fantasy. The idea that a work of art mediated the "presence" of the artist or of the meaning he wished to convey was replaced by the notion that writing is nothing more than a closed system of arbitrary signs.

This theory might be considered quaintly esoteric if it were confined to the ivory tower, but in reality it reflects the larger spiritual crisis of our times. Having unmoored ourselves from our Judeo-Christian roots, we are now forced to create our own makeshift theology from pieces drawn from our cultural legacy. Now that the great secular religions of Marx and Freud have also waned, we are witnessing the kind of religious hunger reported by journalists and writers like Dan Wakefield. But New Age religion and mail-order Christianity are not really interested in confronting the presence of God.

Denis Donoghue's incisive critique of recent literary theory, *Ferocious Alphabets*, illuminates the mystery of presence. "We read to meet the other," Donoghue writes. The author's presence, even as we meet it on the page, emerges out of that most basic human activity, breathing.

> *Breath, the rhythm of taking and expelling breath, represents the only understanding of presence, which persists not by staying in one unchanging form but by committing itself to a moving form as vulnerable as the heartbeat. Our bodily presence in the world is equally vulnerable. The aura which suffuses the idea of dialogue, conversation, communication, and communion arises from the sense of vulnerability in common. Communion is an attempt not to transcend the conditions in which we live upon our breathing, moment by moment, but to assent to them completely.*

We could say much the same thing for the other art forms, by substituting gesture or eye contact, for example, in the place of breath.

For many Christians, the ultimate expression of communion is the Eucharist, where the "sign" and the "signified" become one. Catholics speak of the doctrine of the Real Presence. Every symbolic and metaphoric moment, whether in art or in life, partakes, to some extent, of that sacramental union in which the ordinary is transubstantiated into the extraordinary. Meeting the "Other" can be fearful

and awesome as well as consoling. We often go through life avoiding intimate encounters with the "other," whether that be God or family or friends.

Great art puts us in touch with the presence of the other. Unfortunately, far too much contemporary art seems to have granted the deconstructionists' claims, eschewing presence for the didacticism of ideological correctness or the exercise of formalistic gamesmanship.

On a popular level, one might point to the short-lived "angel craze" of the 1990s as an example of an apparent longing for divine presence. But how many of these comforting angelic visitants perform their traditional function of mediating God's presence? "Fear not"? Not hardly. New Age angels do not bring us divine imperatives or brandish flaming swords; they are the sentimental projections of narcissism gone to seed.

Invoking presence through the careful delineation of a fictional character, or the application of brushstrokes, is an arduous enterprise. In the end it can only be sustained by a belief that there is an unseen but real Presence behind each of our lesser experiences of presence. As George Steiner put it in his seminal book, *Real Presences:* "Any coherent account of the capacity of human speech to communicate meaning and feeling is, in the final analysis, underwritten by the assumption of God's presence."

Flannery O'Connor was once at a literary soirée where the Eucharist was generally admitted to be a powerful symbol. If it's just a symbol, she interjected, "then to hell with it." A tart remark, perhaps, but it cut to the heart of the matter. We hope the writing and art featured in *Image* manifest the courage and the vulnerability of those willing to encounter the presence of the Other.

Base Imitation

Report of fashions in proud Italy,
Whose manners still our tardy apish nation
Limps after in base imitation.
—Shakespeare, *King Richard the Second*

EZRA Pound's famous definition of the artist's task has the elegant simplicity of a scientific formula. "MAKE IT NEW!" Pound commanded, in his habitually imperious manner. Though it has become a commonplace that modern artists have placed too great a value on novelty, the fact remains that each artist—staring at the blank page or screen or canvas—is confronted by the awesome challenge of making something new rather than merely imitating what has gone before.

I have often thought that Pound's dictum might actually be rendered as a scientific formula: $M + I = N$. The first element, to "make" (which in Greek is *poesis*), signifies the creative act itself. That is simple enough. But the imagination cannot operate in a vacuum: it must act upon something. That raises the question of what that something is (the "I" in the equation). I would argue that it encompasses the human condition itself: where we came from, who we are, and where we are going. This brings us to the final term. The result of the imagination acting upon the matter of our humanity is the creation of a unique artifact—an aesthetic form—which is essentially "new." Unless the work of art is new in some vital way, it cannot lay claim to our attention.

Of course, Jews and Christians understand that the human creative act is what J.R.R. Tolkien called "sub-creation." We work with the primary materials God, the Great Artificer, has given us. However, as creatures made in the image and likeness of God, we have been infused with a desire to make new things—the very desire that characterizes the Creator himself.

Why is it, then, that among religious communities in the West today we find so little true creativity and so many cheap knock-offs of pop culture trends and clichés? A full answer to that question would have to take into account the complexities of intellectual and cultural history. Short of such a major investigation, a good starting point would be simply to recognize the magnitude of the problem.

Some of the most egregious examples of the tendency to create Christian clones of secular culture can be found in the evangelical subculture. Evangelical book publishers have discovered a lucrative market in producing genre fiction: romance novels, westerns, techno-thrillers, mysteries, fantasies and sci-fi epics; most of them pallid imitations of Tom Clancy, Zane Grey, Barbara Cartland, and

Tolkien himself. Popular music provides innumerable similar examples. Within six months of the emergence of any new trend or sound in contemporary music, you can expect to find evangelical record labels churning out their own versions. Hence Christian hip-hop and Christian heavy metal.

The relationship between the religious faith of these artists and the vision embodied in their works is extremely tenuous. There may be a didactic lesson in the lyrics or a religious conversion in the novel, but the pleasure afforded by these works stems largely from their genre characteristics. Often it seems that the evangelical consumer is merely comforted by the knowledge that the author/creator is "saved" and therefore OK. The Christian vision is attached to these works like a piece of Scotch tape to a wet sheet of construction paper.

Catholics and mainline Protestants are hardly in a better situation. The decay of liberalism has led to opposite forms of imitation. Convinced that the Judeo-Christian tradition has been dominated by "dead white males," liberal Christians have sought enlightenment and thrills from the East, from C.G. Jung, from neopaganism, witchcraft, and other forms of primitivism. There is less emphasis in these communities on producing specifically Christian music or fiction, but there are dozens of books, workshops, and therapeutic strategies that derive their creative kick from such activities as communing with one's "dark side" and interpreting supposedly mystic symbols such as the Enneagram.

What is missing in these communities is the transformative power of the religious imagination, the ability to search out the operation of God's grace in the complex tangle of our lives.

To be sure, deeply imaginative works of art will almost always be an acquired taste for the relatively few. For one thing, such works place more demands on the mind and heart than most people feel like making. Unfortunately, the dumbing down of society in general has made Christians far more susceptible to the lure of pop culture than was the case in the past. Then there is the economic dimension of this problem. As consumers of culture, Christians will find that the supply will always conform to their demand. But there can be intelligent and honest discussion among people of faith about the problem of facile imitation and the need to encourage the production and appreciation of art that is transfigured by the religious imagination.

It was Jesus, after all, who said: "Behold, I make all things new." And the one form of imitation Christians must undertake is to imitate Him.

Unsolved Mysteries

LIKE most late-twentieth-century American males, I am given to that odd neuralgic habit known as "channel surfing." I take no pride in this confession, but I have noticed that, for all its deleterious effects, the habit occasionally yields unexpected and illuminating insights into the state of American culture. To mix the metaphor, one could say that the channel surfer, like a scientist at a microscope, sees a cross section of our social order.

On my most recent travels across the media waves I have noticed the enormous popularity of such pseudo-documentary programs as *Unsolved Mysteries, Sightings,* and *The Extraordinary.* The range of these shows is astonishing: from UFOs, Bigfoot, and the Loch Ness Monster to telepathic twins, alien abductions, apparitions of the Blessed Virgin Mary, and faith healing. I suppose that these mystery programs, like the scandal mongering *Hard Copy* and its clones, ultimately derive from the same source in tabloid journalism.

But my intention here is not to launch into another sermon on the decadence of popular culture. What interests me is the hunger for mystery that permeates all levels of our culture. Consider the phenomenal success of more sophisticated television programs like *The X-Files*. This show plays (in re-runs now) elegant variations on one standard scenario: two FBI agents, in their crusade for truth about human contact with an alien race, become entangled in a web of disinformation, shadowy conspiracies, and government repression. In episode after episode, agents Mulder and Scully came to the very brink of revelation, only to be thwarted in their quest for truth. Moreover, their enemies are not only bureaucrats, scientists, and businessmen; their own egos and personal obsessions also threaten to corrupt their quest.

The most common visual metaphor in the series is the blinding light—whether from a UFO or just a flashlight—which is too bright for human eyes. Mulder and Scully learn that mystery will not simply yield to aggressive investigation of the rational Enlightenment type. There are times when intuition plays a crucial role, and there are even times when they have to allow the mystery to remain inscrutable.

There is no doubt that *The X-Files* plays on fashionable aesthetics, from paranoia à la Oliver Stone to the dark obscurities of David Lynch's post-modern soap opera *Twin Peaks*. But the success of *The X-Files* is grounded in its subtle understanding of the relationships between mystery, truth, fear, desire, and denial.

The success of *The X-Files* is based on our powerful sense of identification with agents Mulder and Scully. Their passionate desire to penetrate into the heart of mystery, to risk contact with the otherworldly, awakens the same desire in us. Though Mulder and Scully never "solve" their cases, they become guardians of those mysteries, keepers of a flame too bright to look into directly.

With the recent collapse of Enlightenment rationalism—from Marxist social planning to Freudian psychoanalysis—we are once again searching for mystery, for moments of illumination in a world that is larger than ourselves. Though many still look to science as a source of mystery and wonder, it seems to me that scientific discoveries are more than ever pointing our minds in the direction of religious wisdom. If that is true, then there is an enormous opportunity today for a revival of the religious imagination.

The biggest threat to such a revival, however, is the common notion that religious dogma are antithetical to mystery. There is no doubt that religion itself can become rationalized, its mysteries bled dry in abstract theological formulations. But the genius of the Judeo-Christian tradition is that its central dogma *are* mysteries, from the covenant with Abraham to the Trinity, Incarnation, and Resurrection. Church Fathers like Augustine and Athanasius saw their mission not in making these mysteries explicit, but in protecting them from various forms of reductionism.

If one looks at the great religious writers and artists, you will find that nearly all of them were theologically orthodox. Perhaps as artists they had an intuitive understanding of the need for balance between flesh and spirit, concrete form and abstract idea. Dante, Bach, Rembrandt, Hopkins, and T.S. Eliot believed in the mysteries preserved and enshrined by the dogma of the Church. That those mysteries were paradoxical and many-faceted they never doubted.

The alternatives are either to worship mystery for its own sake—

an undertaking that inevitably leads to a vague, unfocused, and subjective vision of the world—or to seek comfort in the pharisaical explicitness of fundamentalism.

Emerson vs. Hawthorne

S INCE the first settlers came to these shores, a Manichean
struggle has raged at the heart of American culture—a struggle
between those who see this country as a new Garden of Eden, full of
endless possibilities, and those who believe that the flawed human
heart and the burdens of history cause us to be permanently exiled
from any worldly paradise.

In my attempts to come to grips with the most recent versions of
this enduring conflict, I have found it helpful to focus on one episode
in particular: the mid-nineteenth-century confrontation between
Ralph Waldo Emerson and Nathaniel Hawthorne. These two literary
giants engaged in this dialectic of American history and brought to
it the full force of their imaginations.

Emerson, who left the Unitarian church because it retained one
too many vestiges of traditional Christianity, might be seen as the
father of the utopian approach to politics and culture. Though

Emerson is known for his concept of self-reliance, few people realize that in his hands this concept has little to do with the relatively innocent tradition of "rugged individualism." At the core of Emerson's thought lies a restless impatience with the restraints inherent in history and human nature. Emerson's philosophical idealism—what one scholar has called "inverted Platonism"—held that the world is the shadow of the mind. Thus Emerson's self-reliant individual defines himself by bringing the world into alignment with the ideas in his mind rather than by attuning himself to an order that transcends him. The end result of this belief is the divinization of the self.

By stressing the self-created individual over against community and history, Emerson contributed to the atomization of American culture. His penchant for abstraction caused him to reject the concrete, sacramental vision of Christianity. Flannery O'Connor wrote that the day Emerson decided he could no longer celebrate Holy Communion was the critical watershed in American history.

Emerson's ideas have been so powerful that in our day they have permeated both conservative and liberal camps. Many conservatives resonate with Emerson's emphasis on self-reliance and enterprise. The type of conservative rhetoric that scorns any form of limits, that touts a vision of an expansive, corporate, technological society, is arguably nothing more than orthodox Emersonianism. On the other hand, it is not at all far-fetched to trace Emerson's role in the development of secular liberalism, the therapeutic mentality, and New Age religiosity. When the divinized self becomes the measure of all things, then restraints and hierarchies—such as the traditional family, sexual morality, and the like—become obstacles that must be eliminated.

Opposing Emerson in his own day was Nathaniel Hawthorne, who embodied a more traditional, Judeo-Christian humanism. Hawthorne's insistence on the reality of evil, the inexorable presence of the past, and a tragic sense of life stood in stark contrast to Emersonian optimism and utopianism. In such novels as *The Blithedale Romance, The Scarlet Letter,* and *The Marble Faun,* Hawthorne

strove to find an authentic American vision through which the traditional, orthodox vision could once again be made relevant.

Though he was deeply disturbed by Emerson's religion of self, with all of its liberalizing tendencies, Hawthorne did not respond by becoming a mere reactionary. Rather, Hawthorne sought to transcend ideology altogether. If he could show the anarchic tendencies of liberalism in *The Blithedale Romance,* he could just as skillfully expose those repressive conservatives, the Puritans, in *The Scarlet Letter.* Again and again, Hawthorne struggled to achieve a more sacramental perspective, which placed the self in relation to the transcendent, and which encompassed a vision of redemptive suffering.

In its essential outlines, the Hawthorne-Emerson struggle foreshadowed our "culture wars" with their increasingly polarized factions. At the same time, Hawthorne's imaginative search exemplifies the religious humanism that can bring healing to a divided culture. Though the recent Hollywood version of *The Scarlet Letter* with Demi Moore as Hester was so far removed from the original that it could be called *Emerson's Revenge,* there are many signs that Hawthorne's spirit is alive and well in some of our finest writers and artists. Along with Hawthorne, these artists gather around the altar that Emerson had turned away from. There they find history, suffering, and the death and resurrection of the self.

Apocalypse Tomorrow

WHEN Jim Jones handed out nine hundred cups of poison-laced Kool-Aid to his followers at Jonestown, Guyana, to what extent was that a religious act—a Black Mass of death and despair? The same question might be asked about David Koresh when he set fire to the Branch Davidian compound in Waco, or those responsible for the truck-bomb that exploded in front of the Murrah Building in Oklahoma City, or the group of Islamic fundamentalists who tried to blow up the World Trade Center in 1993, and who succeeded in that task on September 11, 2001. In each case a fundamentalist strain of religion—whether Christian, Muslim, or a sick variant of the American civil religion—led its devotees to acts of cataclysmic violence.

Were these incidents religious events? I think most people would answer: No, each of those catastrophes was the responsibility of depraved or mentally disturbed individuals who had no conception of authentic religious truth. When one examines the psyches of the perpetrators, their pathologies are legion. And yet it would be wrong to deny that a certain kind of religious sensibility haunted each of these episodes—the religious tradition of apocalyptic expectation or millenarianism. As we try to puzzle out the meanings behind the traumas of Waco and Oklahoma City and 9/11, few of us can avoid the feeling that more acts of apocalyptic violence may be in store.

Visions of the apocalypse tend to emerge when societies undergo huge psychic and cultural dislocations. The advent of apocalyptic consciousness in Judaism, vividly rendered in the Book of Daniel, came around 200 B.C., when conflicts of political and cultural identity had risen to a fever pitch. Similar crises were present when the Book of Revelation was written. Parallels between those times and our own, though they have become hackneyed, retain a core of truth.

There are many who look upon the notion of apocalypse with fear, distaste, or even anger. It is not difficult, for example, to criticize the Hal Lindseys in our midst, religious gnostics who make their living predicting Armageddon in morbid detail while holding out visions of glory and triumph for those who heed their predictions. There is a frame of mind that needs to see massive, utterly evil conspiracies at work in order to account for social disorder and anomie. Of course, secular variants abound, including the left-wing conspiracy theories of otherwise intelligent people like Noam Chomsky and Oliver Stone.

A more subtle attack on the apocalyptic vision was voiced a few years ago in an essay on the Book of Revelation by the writer John Hersey. According to Hersey, Revelation directly contradicts the spirit of the Gospels. By emphasizing a passive waiting for the end of things, Hershey argues, Revelation goes against Christ's command that we serve others in this world. There is a grain of truth here, I think, because one of the paradoxes of the millenarian state of mind is that it can justify either passivity or extreme forms of action—either a waiting for the inevitable or a conscious effort to precipitate the final conflagration. The passivity of some plays into the hands of the violent few.

But I found Hersey's reading of Revelation so superficial that it forced me to rethink the role of the apocalypse, which I suddenly realized had been a small but powerful part of my own faith. Hersey misses the consolation in Revelation and the encouragement for the faithful to remain true to their faith—a faith in the Christ of the Gospels—despite persecution and misunderstanding. For a writer, Hersey is strangely indifferent to the highly charged symbolism of Revelation, the cosmic opera depicting good and evil pushed to their ultimate ends. Apocalyptic literature may be an acquired taste—like opera itself—but through the centuries it has helped many people to understand their own individual struggles against a backdrop of the larger story of God's involvement in history.

Apocalypse is about endings. True, the endtime is often portrayed as a lurid and violent war, but that is because apocalypse is also about judgment, about God's disentangling of good from the evil that has entwined itself through every aspect of life. The imagery of human society uprooted and broken apart serves to remind us just how fragile and artificial our civilization is. In the hands of a novelist like Walker Percy, the apocalyptic tradition has been reimagined and made contemporary. By extrapolating our *fin de siècle* malaise into books like *Love in the Ruins, The Last Gentleman,* and *The Second*

Coming, Percy found a way to diagnose—and judge—the spiritual sicknesses that afflict us.

Perhaps one of the most dangerous ills of modern man is his unwillingness to accept that human life and human societies must come to an end. The resurgence of interest in a pagan, cyclical vision of history may relieve some people of the burden of moral responsibility laid on them by the Judeo-Christian heritage, but in the long run it will end in the kind of despair that hung so heavily on the world into which Christ was born.

Those who take it upon themselves to become the executors of God's judgment—the Osama Bin Ladens of the world—always corrupt and invert the truths they claim to espouse. But that sad fact does not invalidate the humbling and strangely comforting visions of the books of Daniel and Revelation. The apocalypse may tell us of wars in heaven, but it also has another note, one of redemptive joy. The Lion of Judah who comes to judge our souls is also the Lamb of God who will wipe away all our tears.

Going Underground

ONE of the greatest strains in the life of any artist or writer is the constant pressure to promote one's work and to compete in the marketplace. First and foremost there is the stress of economic survival, which for most artists is a lifelong struggle. It is no accident that many creative types dislike the market economy; after all, their "product" is often looked upon as a useless luxury and (in America, at least) there is the not-always-covert feeling that they are little more than freeloaders.

But my guess is that the majority of artists do not resent the market economy so much as the need to advertise themselves and gain public recognition. The private, solitary act of artistic creation is one thing; stepping outside of that inwardness in order to push the "product" is something utterly different. Those who criticize artists as spoiled whiners generally have no conception of this psychic tension.

Artists and writers cope with this tension in a variety of ways. They hire publicists and agents, sign on with galleries, hit the lecture circuit. Often they take matters into their own hands, selling their work out of their studio, or through the Internet, or by going directly to a sympathetic editor. There are some who seem to thrive on self-promotion. The last two hundred years of Western history have tended to support those artists who happily thrust themselves into the limelight. From the Romantics to the High Modernists and beyond, the tradition of the artist as hero and martyr has led to the glorification of the artist as superstar, media prankster, or political protester. From Gauguin's image of himself as a Nietzchean force beyond good and evil to the camera-oriented antics of Andy Warhol, Jeff Koons, and Karen Finley is not that great a leap.

Still, for most artists the tension remains. In the case of artists who are religious believers, the tension, though it may not be greater than that of nonbelievers, at least has an added spiritual dimension. How can one be humble and meek and yet be adept at selling oneself, particularly in a culture that favors the aggressive, media-savvy personality? How does the artist of faith deal with a hostile cultural establishment and not give in to rage or despair?

For some artists the struggle simply becomes too much; they become drop-outs. In a few cases, the experience of burn-out is accompanied by an intense religious experience. For example, a few years ago I came across the writing of an Anglo-American poet named Dunstan Thompson, who was often mentioned in the same breath as Dylan Thomas as one of the most promising poets of his time. After years of behaving like Dylan Thomas, Thompson converted to Christianity and made almost no effort to publish again. After his death one of his friends published a remarkable book of Thompson's poetry, written over the course of decades.

Or take the example of the painter William Congdon (featured in *Image* #14). In the 1950s, Congdon was considered a rising star. He was frequently associated with Jackson Pollock and the Action Painters, and praised by critics like Clement Greenberg and patrons like Peggy Guggenheim. Then, in 1959, after years of inner turmoil and crisis, he was received into the Catholic church and joined a Christian community in Assisi, Italy. Because he stopped promoting his work, for many it seemed that Congdon had just dropped off the face of the earth. But he never stopped painting. Even without the pressure of public attention his work remained at the highest pitch of intensity and brilliance. There is little doubt that Congdon could have been "rediscovered" at any time, but the strength of his religious faith, combined with his seeming betrayal of the mainstream art world, kept most of his former patrons and promoters away.

Though there are some who would call artists like Thompson and Congdon neurotic or anti-social, I cannot see it that way. The decision to take oneself out of the game, it seems to me, can in some instances be an act of courage, rather than of cowardice. Perhaps when these individuals do drop off the face of the earth they go below the surface, into an underground. Not in the sense of Dostoevsky's alienated "Underground Man," but in the manner of the catacombs.

Beneath the clamor of a world that is increasingly giving way to triviality and despair, the religious underground artist pursues beauty for its own sake, as an echo of the prodigal creative energy of the Creator. Like Gerard Manley Hopkins struggling with his own demons and pouring out words in sprung rhythm unheard in his own time, the religious underground artist thinks of God as the first member of his audience. To do this takes a particular kind of courage. Even though it is hidden from view, the work is there, below the surface, like a buried gem or an archaeological trove. It is up to us to find it.

And the Pixel Was Made Flesh

THE advent of the new telecommunications technologies—including the Internet and its primary manifestation, the World Wide Web—has generated a torrent of hype and hyperbole. But even if we were to discount all the euphoric statements that have been made about the wonders of the "electronic global village," the fact remains: we have, willy-nilly, entered the Digital Age. Our most astute cultural observers, whether they are friends or foes of these technologies, agree that the medium of the printed word is giving way to the faster-paced, point-and-click realm of Net-surfing, hypertext, and video-on-demand.

Of course, Marshall McLuhan's prophetic voice told us thirty years ago that "the medium is the message"—that reading, a deeply private and internal experience, was soon to be superseded by the public, in-your-face, immersive experiences of television and computers. Over the years, McLuhan has received his own share of hype (and knew how to generate his own)—but he was essentially right. The medium does have a substantial impact on the message.

What are the implications of this shift from books to digital technology for the future of the Judeo-Christian tradition? If the religious heritage of the West is centered on the primacy of the sacred *books*, and if Christianity understands its savior as the divine *Word*, how will the digitally-reared generations come to perceive God, grace, and the biblical narrative?

I cannot pretend that I have any answers to these questions. On the one hand I have a variety of concerns and fears, while on the other I have a strong instinct not to respond like a Luddite with my head firmly stuck in the sand.

The last major paradigm shift in communications took place in the fifteenth century, with Gutenberg's printing press and the transition from oral culture to literary culture. Both cultures, however, sprang from the spoken word, even if in books the "presence" of the speaking voice was indirect.

In the Greek, *logos* means not only "word" but also the cosmic "reason" that orders the universe. The *logos* emerges out of silence and is spoken into the silence of our hearts and minds, where it continues its ordering work. In the Western tradition, reading demanded an arduous act of imaginative response. The critic Sven Birkerts has spoken of reading as putting us in "deep time"—an austere, one-on-one encounter with the mind of the author.

By contrast, the Internet is like a huge bulletin board or public mural that we can skim across, occasionally dipping in to follow a thought or download an image or sound file. Though it might seem reasonable to say that "text is always text," whether in ink or in the colored pixels of a computer screen, I wonder if that is really so. On the Web the use of "hypertext" links to other subjects is a constant temptation to fly off on tangents. My experience of trying to follow Internet trails is that there are rare occasions when I make significant discoveries but countless episodes where I end up in thickets and cul-de-sacs, wondering how I got there in the first place. Significantly, the piece of software one needs to explore the Web is known as a "browser."

If we lose the mental, emotional, and imaginative discipline of reading, shorten our attention spans even further, fill our minds with trivia, and become adept at manipulating surface images, how prepared will our hearts be to recognize the quiet intimacies of grace? Words are certainly not immutable, but they have more stability than pixels, those infinitely shifting points of light.

Then there is the issue of personal presence and identity. Imagine a computer-generated world of "virtual reality" where you appear to others not as yourself, but as a movie star, or a member of the opposite sex, or Roger Rabbit. Netheads glorify this infinite regression of role-playing, but does this type of posturing offer us more than face-to-face encounters? Meeting "f2f," as the computer generation puts it, is hardly a guarantee of a significant encounter. But with the experience of physical presence—an arch of the eyebrow, a gesticulating hand, a sudden change in the timbre of a voice—we have the opportunity to share ourselves honestly and meaningfully. In reading literature, we focus on the very same details that express individuality and character.

Postmodernists love the Internet because they delight in endless role-playing. Christians, however, are supposed to spend an entire lifetime learning how to take off the many masks we wear in order to meet, and love, a Person.

When a new and powerful technology comes along, the proper response, I feel, is not to deny its existence, but to hedge it around with moral and cultural restraints. We continue to live in the midst of huge arsenals of biological, chemical, and nuclear weapons, but we have dramatized the insanity of their potential use so often that the Bomb no longer looms large in our collective fears. At the risk of sounding like Luddites, we must be willing to utter dire prophecies and sketch out worst-case scenarios. Only then will we be able to inoculate ourselves against the most dangerous tendencies of a new technology.

Religious Humanism: A Manifesto

THE title I've given this essay is half-serious, half-ironic. Religious humanists are, by and large, men and women of letters who command no legions, and who go about their work without much taste for manifestos and movements. Throughout history, religious humanists have manifested a keen awareness of the limits of political action and ideological posturing.

But because we live in a time that is already dominated by strident ideologies and suffering from cultural fragmentation, I feel impelled to articulate more explicitly the central ideas of religious humanism. For this is the strand of the Judeo-Christian tradition that animates *Image.* To my mind, religious humanism offers the best antidote to the ravages of the "culture wars." And since it is so difficult to focus the public's attention in an era of media overload, I am taking the risk of championing religious humanism as though it were a "cause." In recent years I have encountered hundreds of thoughtful Christians and Jews who have been struggling to embody a vision of religious humanism in their lives and in their work. Perhaps by giving a name to this vision, we can speak more clearly and forcefully to the world around us. That, at least, is my hope.

In the history of the West, religious humanism has made only infrequent appearances and has rarely occupied center stage. It is a mode of thought that tends to arise when religious and cultural cohesion is threatened by social and intellectual upheavals. It is arguable, however, that religious humanists are like *tzaddikim,* the legendary thirty six good men (whose identities are known only to God) celebrated by the Hasidic Jewish thinkers. If any of the *tzaddikim* were to die and not be replaced, the Hasidim believed, the world would come to an end.

What do I mean by religious humanism? The theologian Max Stackhouse provided a simple but suggestive definition. "Humanity," Stackhouse wrote, "cannot be understood without reference to God; and neither God nor God's revelation can be understood except through the lens of thought and experience."

On the face of it, the term "religious humanism" seems to suggest a tension between two opposed terms—between heaven and earth. But it is a creative, rather than a deconstructive, tension. Perhaps the best analogy for understanding religious humanism comes from the Christian doctrine of the Incarnation, which holds that Jesus was both human and divine. This paradoxical meeting of these two natures is the pattern by which we can begin to understand the many dualities we experience in life: flesh and spirit, nature and grace, God and Caesar, faith and reason, justice and mercy.

When emphasis is placed on the divine at the expense of the

human (the conservative fault), Jesus becomes an ethereal authority figure who is remote from earthly life and experience. When he is thought of as merely human (the liberal error), he becomes nothing more than a superior social worker or popular guru.

The religious humanist refuses to collapse paradox in on itself. This has an important implication for how he or she approaches the world of culture. Those who make a radical opposition between faith and the world hold such a negative view of human nature that the products of culture are seen as inevitably corrupt and worthless. On the other hand, those who are eager to accommodate themselves to the dominant trends of the time baptize nearly everything, even things that may not be compatible with the dictates of the faith. But the distinctive mark of religious humanism is its willingness to adapt and transform culture, following the dictum of an early Church Father, who said that "Wherever there is truth, it is the Lord's." Because religious humanists believe that whatever is good, true, and beautiful is part of God's design, they have the confidence that their faith can transform the works of culture. Transformation, rather than rejection or accommodation, constitutes the heart of the religious humanist's vision.

One might ask why the incarnational balance of the human and the divine is not so obvious as to be universally accepted. The truth is that human beings find it difficult to live with paradox. It is far easier to seek a resolution in one direction or the other; indeed, making such a choice often seems to be the most principled option.

Perhaps the best illustration of religious humanism I've come across can be found in the film *The Mission.* It tells the story of the Jesuit missionaries who attempted to penetrate the rainforests of

Brazil and bring the faith to the remote tribes. As the film opens, we see a missionary ejected from the tribe in a literal and gruesomely ironic fashion: tied to a cross and sent over the edge of a huge waterfall. This missionary had evidently tried to preach to the tribesmen and had been rejected. But the Jesuit played by Jeremy Irons enters a clearing near where the tribe lives, sits down on a rock, and begins playing an oboe. This simple gesture, which appealed directly to the humanity of the tribespeople, enabled them to recognize what was human in him. They arrive with their spears raised but they soon accept him and, ultimately, convert to Christianity.

With all these references to paradox and ambiguity the objection might be made that I am speaking in quintessentially liberal terms, refusing to state my allegiance to the particularities of the faith. In fact, the majority of religious humanists through the centuries have been deeply orthodox, though that does not mean they don't struggle with doubt or possess highly skeptical minds. The orthodoxy of the great religious humanists is something that liberals tend to ignore or evade; it doesn't tally with their notion that dogma are somehow lifeless and repressive. But dogma are nothing more—or less—than restatements of the mysteries of faith. Theological systems can become calcified and unreal—they can, in short, give rise to "dogmatism"—but dogma exist to protect and enshrine mystery. Flannery O'Connor, one of the great religious humanists of the twentieth century, wrote of the effect her faith had on her writing: "There is no reason why fixed dogma should fix anything that the writer sees in the world. On the contrary, dogma [are] an instrument for penetrating reality. Christian dogma is about the only thing left in the world that surely guards and respects mystery." In a similar vein one need only think of the modern Jewish thinkers (Martin Buber and Emmanuel Levinas among them) who have joined their passionate love of the Hasidic tradition to such modern philosophic schools as personalism and existentialism.

So we arrive at yet another paradox: that the religious humanist combines an intense (if occasionally anguished) attachment to orthodoxy with a profound spirit of openness to the world. This helps to explain why so many of the towering figures of religious humanism—from Gregory of Nyssa, Maimonides, Dante and Erasmus to Fyodor Dostoevsky, T.S. Eliot, and Flannery O'Connor—have been writers possessed of powerful imaginations. The intuitive powers of the imagination can leap beyond the sometimes leaden abstractions with which reason must work. Because the imagination is always searching to move from conflict to a higher synthesis, it is the natural ally of religious humanism, which struggles to assimilate the data of the world into a deeper vision of faith.

The transformative power of religious humanism enables it to balance the changing circumstances of history with what T.S. Eliot called the "permanent things." One of the most luminous explanations of this balance was written by John Henry Newman, a Victorian theologian who eventually became a cardinal in the Catholic church. His book on the "development of doctrine" argues that the unfolding of history enables us to see—and respond to—new facets of meaning in the ancient dogma. Newman's concept of doctrinal development has been cited by many scholars as the underlying inspiration for the Second Vatican Council, with its stress on the need for a dialogue between the church and the modern world.

Since the roots of religious humanism go so far back into the European past, a skeptic might wonder whether such a mode of thought has ever been deeply grafted onto American culture. After all, America is still a relatively young nation and its Puritan and pragmatic strains—neither particularly hospitable to humanism— are ingrained in our history. Without intending to scant the contributions of earlier religious thinkers, I believe that the leading American representatives of religious humanism have been imaginative writers. Nathaniel Hawthorne's insistence on the reality of evil, the inexorable presence of the past, and a tragic sense of life stood in stark contrast to Emerson's optimism and utopianism. Throughout his career, Hawthorne struggled to achieve a more sacramental perspective, which placed the self in relation to the transcendent, and which encompassed a vision of redemptive suffering. It is possible to draw a direct line from Hawthorne to such modern American writers as T.S. Eliot, Flannery O'Connor, Walker Percy, Richard Rodriguez, and Annie Dillard.

Despite the harsh cultural climate in which we live, a new generation of religious humanists is making its presence known. The new religious humanists have a number of things going for them.

Now that the Baby Boomers have arrived at middle age, fully aware for the first time of their mortality and concerned about their children's moral and physical well-being, we have witnessed a wave of interest in religion, ranging from the pursuit of New Age pantheism to a nostalgia for traditional rites and moral codes. Indeed, religious humanism must compete with the Wal-Mart of spiritual and therapeutic nostrums available today. Even if much of this can be discounted as sentimental religiosity, a spirit of openness has emerged.

There is no "school" of religious humanism, no centralized office or publication that represents it to the worlds of politics or the media, no platform with readily identifiable political planks. However, there are subtle but powerful threads that link many of the most distinguished minds of our time. In philosophy Alasdair MacIntrye and Charles Taylor have brought the existence of God and the idea of "the good" back into serious discussion. Theologians such as the American Jesuit Avery Dulles, the German Lutheran Wolfhart Pannenberg, and the late Hans Urs von Balthasar and his disciples have demonstrated that faithfulness to the ancient teachings of the church can inspire nuanced and creative thought. There are also a growing number of scholars who have been meditating on the relationship between religion and science, including Stanley Jaki, John Polkinghorne, and Langdon Gilkey.

One clear lesson that these thinkers have learned from the culture wars is that the process of politicization endangers the ability of religion to permeate and renew the very culture that is being fought over. The culture wars might be likened to two gardeners who spend all their time spraying rival brands of pesticide, while forgetting to water the plants and fertilize the soil. Perhaps the most frightening thing about this syndrome is that it seems to betoken a pervasive despair about the very possibility of cultural renewal. To cite just one example of this from my personal experience: the vast majority of conservatives I have encountered are firmly convinced that almost nothing of value has been produced in Western culture for over a hundred years. There is an element of simple Philistinism here, but there is also the despair of those who can only look backward.

Yet another paradox of religious humanism is that it combines a tragic sense of life—an awareness of our fallenness and the limits of human institutions—with a strain of persistent hope. T.S. Eliot once said that there are no lost causes because there are no gained causes. The religious humanist refuses to give in to apocalyptic fears, believing that grace is always available, and that the life-giving soil of culture is often seeded with suffering. If, as I believe, faith and imagination are the two primary sources of culture, then even in the darkest time it is possible to make poems and prayers out of our travails.

The new religious humanists know that culture shapes and informs politics far more powerfully than the other way around. They recognize that symbolism, imagery, and language play a crucial role in forming attitudes and prejudices, and they have devoted themselves to nourishing the imaginative life. At a time when the model of Enlightenment rationalism is crumbling under the weight of post-modern cynicism and nihilism, the religious imagination can speak meaningfully into the void.

In fact, it is the novelists, poets, artists, and composers who are at the heart of the resurgence of religious humanism in our time.

Image exists to chronicle this renaissance and to communicate it to a larger audience. This mission is all the more important because there is a serious "perception gap" in the West today: many people—whether religious or secular—don't know about this renaissance or, what is worse, don't want to believe it is possible. Perhaps that is why religious humanists need to be willing to stand up and issue an occasional manifesto.

In an essay on Christian humanism published in *Image,* the comparative literature scholar Virgil Nemoianu singles out the two virtues he believes to be most essential to religious humanism: courage and hope. These are indeed high and holy virtues, like twin mountain peaks. Thinking about these virtues we might do well to compare ourselves to Dante the pilgrim, who looks up to the shining stars of heaven from his dark wood. We may not be able to attain these peaks without a painful effort of trial and error. But we can keep them ever in our sight.

Master Narrative

OVER the years, my wife and I have tried to make a point of reading aloud to our children at bedtime. As anyone who has done this will tell you, children constitute an audience that is, more often than not, acutely sensitive to nuance and detail, and utterly exacting when it comes to narrative coherence. This has become especially evident to me on those occasions when I have attempted (with a rather naïve foolhardiness) to spin out a series of original stories for my kids. For all the hype about computers providing children with "interactive" learning experiences, there is nothing like telling a child a story for interactivity. My kids are polite enough to raise their hands when they have some penetrating question to ask about plot, character, or setting, but I know that my imagination is flagging when their hands shoot up with every other sentence. If I leave something out of the story, or commit the sin of inconsistency, these fierce critics won't let me proceed until I've revised the narrative. Oddly enough, they never attempt to take over the storytelling. They are convinced that I have the authority to tell the tale, but they insist that I live up to the complete story that they know exists somewhere inside me. It's enough to give me a serious case of performance anxiety.

When children fall (as they must) from innocence into the ambiguous world of adulthood, they often lose their intense attachment to literary and religious narratives as guiding principles in their lives. Full of their newfound physical and mental powers, young adults begin to think that they are writing their own scripts. But there comes the time which Dante described as the "dark wood," mid-way along our path in life, when we realize that we have lost a sense of the story of our lives. In *The Divine Comedy* Dante the pilgrim-poet recovers the story that began with the vision of a beautiful girl named Beatrice; that personal and particular story, rooted in time and place, becomes joined with the cosmic narrative of salvation.

According to postmodern intellectuals, the West is no longer undergirded by the Judeo-Christian story that had guided it—and its great artists, like Dante—for nearly two millennia. These same theorists argue that the modern "master narratives" of Marx and Freud—the secular replacements for the Judeo-Christian story—have also lost their capacity to give meaning to our lives.

This "storyless" moment is welcomed by the postmodernists because they believe that any master narrative is totalitarian. As Robert Royal has written in *The New Religious Humanists: A Reader*, "The postmodern strategy usually denies . . . 'master narratives' in favor of *petites histoires*, that is, personal stories as the only locus of rich meaning open to us. In this view, all the old *grands récits* . . . are dangerous totalizing and potentially terroristic illusions."

Any casual survey of the arts today would reveal that our novels, films, and paintings are geared almost exclusively toward the *petites histoires* rather than the *grands récits.* Where can one find artists now who have the aesthetic ambitions of an Eliot, a Joyce, or a Pound? The majority of postmodern artists believed that in abandoning the master narrative of faith, they would be free to tell the personal stories that reveal the unvarnished truth. When postmodern art refers to the old master narratives, those references are ironic and detached, like inscriptions from an ancient temple whose deity has been long since forgotten.

The question arises: How satisfied are we with the *petites histoires?* Have these small canvases provided us with the meaning and order to bring about a saner, more humane society? Or could it be that these works of art bear an unsettling resemblance to our divided social fabric: lonely, alienated fragments that have seemingly given up the search for a meaningful relationship to the whole?

The resurgence of interest in traditional religion that has manifested itself in various ways in our culture would seem to indicate a desire to recover the great master narrative of the West. The problem is that many people are trying to appropriate individual chapters of that story—from angels and saints to the Book of Genesis to Gregorian chant—rather than to hear the unabridged version.

Of course, literature and art at their best can forge profound imaginative links between the *petites histoires* and the *grands récits,* between the story of the individual soul's pilgrimage and the divine comedy.

There is one great advantage to the faith that the late Walker Percy called "the Jewish-Christian thing," and it is simply this: the story is not over. While we know that the story has a comedic ending (in the sense of Dante's *commedia),* neither our individual nor our collective destinies are predetermined. We are charged with the responsibility of renewing the story, and finding our own connections to it. When the Church's versions of the master narrative become too narrow and triumphalistic, we are called upon to expand the story so that it is more inclusive and humble. When secularism and relativism threaten to empty the faith of content and contour, we must evoke the moral and spiritual boundaries that can guide us through troubled times.

But this process of revision can only take place if we are committed to telling and retelling the *whole* story, not just the bits we think are relevant or fulfilling. Children have an instinctive aversion to leaving anything out of a story. Indeed, it is children's passionate belief in the existence of a master narrative that makes them the heirs of the kingdom.

The Artist as Prophet

AT the 1997 *Image* conference—a conference that addressed the theme "Beyond the Culture Wars"—one of the liveliest question-and-answer sessions took place after James Davison Hunter's talk. Hunter, a sociologist who helped define the term "culture wars," devoted much of his talk to the relationship between the artist and the larger community. He suggested that in order to avoid the conflicts that have often pitted the art world against various sectors of the public, artists should develop a more profound sense of how they might serve the community.

Despite the fact that the majority of people in the audience were churchgoing folk (and thus predisposed to moral and communal concerns), many of those who asked questions after Hunter's talk bristled at the idea that the artist should make his or her work serve the community and any standards the community might set up for acceptable art. This would constitute an intolerable infringement on artistic freedom, they argued, and would lead to art that was so sanitized as to be indistinguishable from propaganda. But there were also many in the audience who sympathized with Hunter's call, noting that artists who have touted creative autonomy as the supreme value have in fact produced work that is pointless, degrading, and obscene—art that is harmful to the community.

Clearly, Hunter's remarks prompted yet another round of an age-old debate, a controversy that the philosopher Jacques Maritain called the perennial struggle between Art and Prudence. From the anxieties of Plato's philosopher kings to the latest congressional harrumphing about the National Endowment for the Arts, the conflict between the creative freedom of the artist and the public good has been vexing and divisive.

Image, being a journal of the arts *and* religion, would seem to have an uneasy foot in both camps. How do we approach such issues? One analogy that has helped us to put this conflict into perspective is that of seeing the artist as prophet.

Like the biblical prophet, the artist is often an outsider, one who stands apart and delivers a challenge to the community. The prophets of old employed many of the same tricks used by writers and artists: lofty rhetoric, apocalyptic imagery, biting satire, lyrical evocations of better times, and subversive irony. To be sure, the true prophet came not to proclaim his own message, but that of the Lord.

Being a prophet was, and is, a hazardous occupation; the possibility of stoning is always present. Prophets have been called disturbers of the peace, revolutionaries, traitors, and babbling madmen. The Bible itself contains stories of many false prophets— charlatans who sought the prophetic mantle but who had no contact with God. But the Bible is also grounded in the truths found in those twin sources of inspiration known as "the law and the prophets."

Flannery O'Connor, who often spoke of the "prophetic poet," was delighted to discover in the *Summa Theologiae* of St. Thomas Aquinas a powerful defense of prophecy and its relationship to the imagination. Contrary to those who dismiss prophecy (and art) for being subjective, St. Thomas notes that prophecy "first and chiefly consists in knowledge, because prophets know things that are far removed from man's knowledge." While God delivers the message, St. Thomas says, the prophet's mind must be elevated by imaginative readiness to receive and then transmit that message. The divine afflatus does not cancel out the human imagination, but raises it to visionary heights.

This passage from the *Summa* is the source from which O'Connor derived her description of the artist as "the realist of distances." The artist and the prophet bring far things near; they somehow bring the urgencies of the eschatological realm into the mundane world of the here and now. That sudden shift in perspective can be disorienting and disturbing. At the same time it can be a deeply moral act. The strains of Puritanism and pragmatism that run deep in the American psyche have always led to a fear of art's willingness to probe the "distances" that lie enshrouded in mystery and ambiguity. That is why school boards and political action committees routinely fail to see the difference between pornography and the writings of Toni Morrison, or between exploitative rubbish like *Showgirls* and serious films like *Breaking the Waves*.

To speak of the artist as a prophet is to confer praise. But it is important to remember that even in biblical times the prophet was not completely independent of the community. Prophets might have been more free to speak their minds than the average members of society, but they were not autonomous. The office of prophet was not the same as that of priest or king, and the prophet had no right to arrogate those roles to himself. Of course, that sort of aesthetic aggrandizement has been all too common in the modern era. Sadly, the defenders of the NEA—and the arts in general—cannot articulate an argument that moves beyond the idea of artistic autonomy.

The prophet and the artist may seek to disturb the existing order of things, but they should do so in the name of a deeper order, not in the name of their own genius. The artist will serve the community best not by worrying about either his own autonomy or the community's immediate concerns but by remaining open to the transcendent sources of order. By keeping an eye fixed on the distances, the artist will do justice to both art and community.

Liturgical Art and its Discontents

FROM time to time the editors of *Image* are asked why we don't cover liturgical art in our pages. It's a good question. Since *Image* is a journal of "the arts and religion" it would seem only natural for it to focus on liturgical art, which acts as a bridge linking the journal's two themes.

Actually, we've come close a few times. Several artists covered in our pages have had their works displayed in churches and synagogues—sometimes permanently, but more often on a temporary basis. These encounters between artists and worshiping communities have not always been happy.

Liturgical art is an important, but often neglected, topic. Those of us who worship every Saturday or Sunday have to live with liturgical art in one fashion or another, whether we go to the plainest meeting house or the most extravagantly ornate baroque cathedral. Moreover, churches and synagogues constitute significant architectural presences on our public squares—these buildings speak directly to the intersection between faith and culture.

Yet another reason to pay attention to liturgical art is that so much of it is either banal, controversial, or ugly. Nearly everyone has a collection of stories about their favorite liturgical art nightmares: dreary churches that look like roller skating rinks, lumpy sculptures that were better left on the potter's wheel, felt banners with sentimental mottoes in Day-Glo colors.

At the other end of the aesthetic spectrum are the controversies that involve art of a high order. There are a depressingly large number of anecdotes about the failure of talented (and devout) artists to find churches interested in commissioning or using their work.

Of course, liturgical art isn't limited to the visual arts. There is also the artistry of language that goes into biblical translations and the spoken rites of the church. As Kathleen Norris and others have pointed out, the ancient precept of the church says that the *lex orandi,* the order of prayer, helps to shape and define the *lex credendi,* the order of belief. As Norris reminds us, the crisis in liturgy is not centered in the debates over inclusive language and other such political issues, but in the sheer mediocrity and dullness of the words we speak in church. Nowadays the guardians of the church's language are not poets but professional "liturgical consultants" and activists whose background is more likely to be in sociology than in literature. Under such a regime, metaphor and mystery have given way to ideology and condescending ideas about how to make language accessible to the people in the pews.

The subject of liturgical art will always be tangled in a number of subtle aesthetic issues. Because it is art with a *purpose*—as an aid to

worship—liturgical art subordinates the free play of the imagination
to a specific end. Having to serve two masters—the intrinsic dictates
of art and the needs of a worshipping community—liturgical art
often becomes mired in contention and confusion. Can a complicated work of art that evokes in the viewer a savoring of irony,
allusion, and form be conducive to the spiritual single-mindedness
of prayer? To put it differently, can one really *pray* in Michelangelo's
Sistine Chapel? These and a host of related questions rarely get the
attention they deserve.

So, why doesn't *Image*
cover this range of
important issues relating to
liturgical art? My answers
to this question won't satisfy
everyone; they don't even
completely satisfy *me*. But
I'll share them with you
nonetheless.

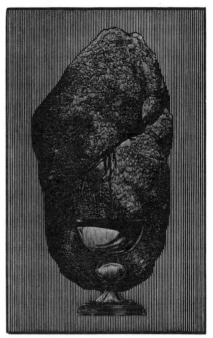

Too many efforts to
relate religion and the arts
have stumbled because they
attempt to channel the
imagination into pious
patterns. At the root of this failure is an underlying fear of the
imagination itself—a force that can't be tamed or made to fit into
comforting, predictable categories. Believers who fear the imagination prefer art that doesn't stray too far from the church porch; they
want to see things they already know gussied up with ornaments and

flourishes. But art at its highest pitch tries to tell us things we don't know, or have forgotten, and that can be unsettling. Also, the majority of our waking hours are not spent in church, but in the world. And if religion is too important to be confined to church services, then so is art that grapples with religious themes.

Image tries to maintain a delicate balance: the editors believe that art should nurture faith, but at the same time we explore art that is not subordinated to the liturgical needs of a particular church or community.

We hope that the work featured in *Image* will have a profound and beneficial impact on liturgical art. Jacques Maritain once wrote: "Religious art is not a thing that can be isolated from art itself, from the general movement of an age: isolate it, and it grows corrupt, becomes dead letter." If that's true, then *Image* may already be making a significant contribution to the enhancement of liturgical art by focusing on the larger movements of our time.

A new journal, one that focuses on liturgical art, is desperately needed. Meanwhile, *Image* will cultivate its own garden and hope that its influence on liturgical art, however indirect, is for the good.

Patron Saints

I once heard a story about the late Walker Percy that seems to illustrate the plight of so many struggling artists down through the ages. Percy graduated from medical school in the 1940s but soon came down with tuberculosis and had to spend a couple years in a sanatorium. During that time he underwent a profound intellectual and religious conversion and decided to become a writer, first of philosophical essays and later of novels. When, a few years later, he moved to the small town of Covington, Louisiana, he went to the local barber shop. Because news traveled quickly in Covington, the barber had already heard the new resident referred to as "Dr. Percy." So as Percy settled into the barber's chair, the barber said to him: "Dr. Percy, what kind of medicine do you practice?" Percy replied that he was no longer a practicing doctor. The barber then asked him what kind of work he was doing. Percy said: "I'm a writer." After a moment's pause and with a skeptical expression on his face, the barber said: "But Dr. Percy, what do you *really* do?" Percy thought for a minute and said: "Nothing." This response satisfied the barber completely.

I would venture a guess that a hefty percentage of the population at any given moment feels—whether consciously or subconsciously—that writers and artists are people who have discovered a number of creative ways to do nothing at all. This prejudice is closely related to the perennial question about the "usefulness" of art. Ironically, one of the glories of art—that it creates fictions, little lies or "nothings"—may also be one of its greatest liabilities.

Except for the tiny fraction of people who make a living in the arts, most artists are forced to look for day jobs and join in the hunt for one kind of patron or another, whether that be a gallery or a publisher or a collector. It's a difficult, messy process, made worse by another popular assumption—that suffering is a prerequisite for great art.

Every artist wants a patron, but no one wants to be patronized. Undoubtedly the history of artist/patron relationships is strewn with tempestuous conflicts and betrayals. Nonetheless, enlightened patrons play an enormously important role in the creation of enduring art and literature. A sensitive and courageous patron can do much more than simply provide financial and emotional support for the artist. The great patrons educate public taste, refresh the roots of culture, and often serve as the first biographers and critics on the scene.

In my fifteen years as fundraiser for *Image* I've learned a great deal about the state of patronage in America, at least as far as the nexus of religion and the arts is concerned. I've found that institutions such as churches, universities, and foundations are, more often than not, timid and confused. The institutional church hasn't been a serious patron of the arts for a couple centuries now, and it hasn't been doing much to make up for lost time. Powerful, arresting art is simply too controversial to please everyone in the pews, and so the lowest common denominator usually wins out.

While there are a few exemplary foundations today that support the making of original art, most foundations have become bureaucratized. They tend to give money to universities and opera houses with huge budgets and marquee names—another symptom of the American passion for bigness.

In the realm of religious philanthropy the news is mixed. While some foundations have begun to recognize the role that art plays in the spiritual life, others have yet to catch on. One of the major foundations in religious philanthropy has just dropped its program for giving to projects that unite religion and the arts. Given the explosion of interest in this area, it's difficult to understand the timing of that decision.

Arguably, the academy is the largest patron of the arts these days because it employs poets, painters, and other artists as professors. This is a mixed blessing, since many such artists, particularly at small liberal arts colleges, are teaching full course loads and are desperate to get into the studio or to the word processor. There's also the danger, pointed out by Dana Gioia and others, that the academic setting can become too isolated and incestuous, too far removed from the outside world to remain vital and relevant.

Individuals can be more decisive and visionary than institutions, but many people with substantial means don't make the connection between their faith and the arts. For some the problem is compartmentalization: they will go to SoHo or Santa Fe to purchase art and then go to church, but it may never occur to them to link these two experiences. For others the obstacle is art itself: they just don't see the point.

As I have struggled with this subject, I find myself returning again and again to a thoughtful essay by the New York artist Makoto Fujimura on how people of faith should think about the value of art. Entitled "The Extravagance of God," it begins with the story of Mary, the sister of Martha and Lazarus, anointing Christ with a pint of pure nard—which was worth about a year's wages. Judas Iscariot objects, wondering why this expensive perfume could not be sold and the proceeds given to the poor.

Fujimura argues that the arts—which require so much investment in training, mastery, and production costs—echo that extravagant gesture of Mary. However virtuous Judas' concern for the poor may be, it still misses something crucial about the divine economy. Christ endorses the prodigality of Mary's act: "She has done a beautiful thing to me. I tell you the truth, wherever the gospel is preached throughout the world, what she has done will also be told, in memory of her...."

Too often in the church today it is Judas who wins the debate, relegating art to the status of a luxury believers cannot afford. But our God is the God of extravagant gestures, the one who made something out of nothing, and the artist has the dignity—and the burden—of being able to echo that act of creativity.

Bearing the Image

I N the ten years since *Image* began publication we've never reflected publicly on our name. Since this issue [#22] marks our tenth anniversary, it seems appropriate to revisit the impulse that launched—and named—the journal.

We chose *Image* for the same reason that anyone selects a good name or title, because it has multiple levels of meaning and connotation, most of which speak directly to our central purpose. Our name alludes not only to the image-making capacity of the artist, but also to the biblical depiction of the God who made man and woman in his own image and likeness. Given our focus on the intersection between art and religious faith—a faith that emerges out of story and symbol, myth and metaphor—*Image* seemed an obvious choice.

And yet we live in an age that is image-saturated and image-driven: our high-tech media and feverish consumerism constantly threaten to empty images of their resonance and depth, leaving us in the no-man's-land between cynicism and despair. We've come a long way from the culture of the Second Commandment, which recognized the human tendency to turn images into idols, but which also dignified man by depicting him as the image of God-the-Maker. At present, the image is being reduced to a few, second-rate modes— the commercial, the sentimental, the ironic. So, at the beginning of the twenty-first century, it seems reasonable to ask how our culture's images might be revitalized.

In his illuminating contribution to the symposium on "The State of the Arts" in this issue, Scott Cairns outlines an aesthetic that sounds a note of hope—a note that we believe has sounded in the pages of *Image* for the past ten years. Cairns argues that we are experiencing a renaissance of sacramental poetry (though his words apply to all of the arts). The word "sacramental" is bandied about rather vaguely these days, but Cairns's use of the analogy is precise: a sacrament, he notes, is not merely a symbol or remembrance of something absent, but actually effects what it represents. In Cairns's words: "The new poetry, a poetry which employs language as *agency and power* rather than merely as *name for another and prior thing,* demands that it be read and re-read, and poked, and puzzled over as an *event of its own.* The new poem is not about a thing; it is a thing."

Cairns, along with a growing number of writers and scholars, believes that postmodern thought, for all its flaws and dead-ends, has had a salutary effect in shattering many of the brittle certainties of a Christendom that had lost touch with its spiritual roots. Many postmodernists have argued that we cannot really know anything, that we can never experience "presence," only the "absence" of a meaning that forever eludes us. But Cairns sees good coming out of this postmodern "troubling" because it has encouraged artists to create art that respects the fleeting nature of presence. Sacramental art, with its stress on agency, on artist and audience coming together in an act of joint discovery, enables us to experience presence, if only in what T.S. Eliot called "hints and guesses." The poet and critic Allen Tate called this aesthetic the "symbolic imagination" and rightly pointed to Dante as one of its greatest exemplars.

It is important, however, that we approach the idea of presence in a paradoxical, rather than a literal, sense. The paradox lies in this: we can experience presence—one might just as easily say *grace*—when art approximates the leap of faith, when it dares to place us directly inside an act of discovery. The risk of imagination, like the risk of faith, instills fear in those who believe we can only be saved by rational propositions. But the paradoxical truth is that unless we learn how to live in that risk-taking leap of faith, we will lose touch with the meaning of those propositions.

Of course, the opposite danger is that when we abandon the concrete particulars—of history or theology or human experience— we float off into a vagueness that lacks an anchor in reality. As I've argued elsewhere, religious dogma are not really propositions, but symbolic mysteries. They should neither be explained to death nor left behind as merely "repressive" stumbling blocks. Only when we maintain such a balanced perspective—a perspective I've called religious humanism—can we go about the task of renewing our culture.

Art, at its highest pitch, always aspires to a condition of sacramental agency. After a century of secularism, in which art sought to find a grounding in science, whether that be psychology or economics or biology, a growing number of artists in the West are turning back to faith as the proper grounding and analogy for the imagination's work. *Image* was founded in order to provide a forum for these artists and writers. Along with our annual conferences, summer workshops, and—we hope—an artists' colony, *Image* will continue its mission of renewal.

A Theology of Erosion

LAST year, while driving south out of the San Luis Valley of Colorado, with the great humpbacked Sangre de Cristo mountain range to my left, I had a sudden epiphany about why I've come to love New Mexico so much. Up to that moment I had formulated my passion for New Mexico in more or less traditional terms: the quality of light, the stark grandeur of the high desert, the haunting work created by the many artists who had come to the state and been permanently bitten by its beauty, the ancient history of three cultures—Native American, Hispanic, and Anglo—that had met, fought, and ultimately mingled there. But it wasn't until somewhere between Tres Piedras and Española that I realized what I most love about the state, and that is erosion.

I know that New Mexico does not have a monopoly on landscapes marked by erosion, but in an indefinable way the state's history and culture seem to find an "objective correlative" in the exposed and corrugated look of arroyos and river beds carved out of soft stone and mud by wind, water, and time. At least that's how I've come to see it.

Though the Native American and Hispanic cultures began their relationship in conflict, both developed a deep-seated knowledge of tragedy and loss, something that their religious traditions had prepared them to understand. This knowledge goes beyond mere endurance and survival; it touches on what the great Basque philosopher Miguel de Unamuno called "the tragic sense of life." From ancient myths of gods in conflict to the disfigured and bloody Spanish crucifixes, these two cultures have never strayed far from the knowledge that suffering shapes and defines our humanity. And it's just possible that the Anglo culture, which began its conquest of the West in typically triumphalistic fashion, has been touched by that tragic sense of life—I think of the years of harsh frontier life, the Civil War (which had a poignant New Mexico chapter), and even the dark legacy of the Los Alamos labs and the Trinity nuclear test site.

I find the eroded landscape of New Mexico to be a perfect analogue for the tragic sense of life. Even the tradition of adobe construction contributes to this sense, because adobe is a fragile material that needs constant tending and renewal. Mud becomes brick but it can so easily revert to mud again. When compared to the rationalistic optimism that came out of the Enlightenment, with its visions of conquering nature and remaking human society, the feminine concavity of the eroded land bespeaks a humbler vision, one less prone to vaulting ambition. Exposed and vulnerable, the rippled hills are worn away by the forces of nature, but what remains is at least as important as what is lost. It is not so much a metaphor of passive endurance as it is of feminine strength, of a beauty shaped by the pains of birth and death. As all mothers know, birth itself is like death—overwhelming, inevitable, fraught with uncertainty. Here, too, adobe provides another feminine analogy, since adobe structures have many curves but few right angles. C.S. Lewis once said that compared to God we are all feminine; no place on earth conveys that better to me

than the landscape and culture of New Mexico.

One contemporary sculptor who has built this fascination with concavity and erosion into his work is Stephen de Staebler (featured in *Image* #2 and #37), whose stone and bronze creations often have the look of ancient monumental statues worn away by time. When asked about this aspect of his work, de Staebler said: "I want to express the quality of erosion in the loss of limbs over time and the rooting of the figure to the earth in time, so that it becomes in its own way an extension of earth, which we are.... So what you see here is this feeling of an eroded separation from something larger in time.... I hope that for the person who isn't too literal this will also have the connotation of being connected in time to creation."

America is a place that has yet to come to terms with tragedy. Our civil religion is based on the idea of a "city on a hill," a *novus ordo seclorum* ("new order of the ages") that will escape the clutches of the tragic past. It's an energetic, forward-looking vision, one that has fueled a great deal of social progress. But it is also a form of arrested adolescence, a state of collective denial that detaches us from reality. Political discourse today, whether of left or right, never speaks of paradox or the tragic conflict of competing goods, only of the bright futures that free enterprise or social reconstruction will bring. Politics itself now seems like a branch of the self-help industry—the source of therapeutic policy.

For me, the land and the history of New Mexico provide a different perspective from which to view social and personal affairs. Weathered rocks and weathered faces remind us that we should not move through time as conquerors, but as suffering servants.

In Defense of Irony

I RONY, it seems, is the hot topic of the moment. The trigger for this spate of op-eds and Sunday arts-section essays is the recent publication of a book by a graduate student at Yale University. Nearly all of the reviewers and commentators treated this young man's book the way my kids treat a box of breakfast cereal: on opening it, they reach down past the main contents of the package to pluck out the toy at the bottom. In the case of this book, the "toy" is the argument that America is suffering from a pervasive attitude of irony.

Nearly all the commentators agree on the essential features of this postmodern affliction: irony is a form of intense self-conscious-ness—a knowing, cynical mistrust of institutions and shared truths. Out of this jaded sensibility comes the ironist's twisted sense of humor, based on the conviction that everything is derivative. The ironist delights in creating a stream of joking allusions, "quoting," as it were, from the cultural baggage of history. "Been there; done that"

might be the only words in the credo of the postmodern ironist. Jerry
Seinfeld's late, eponymous sitcom is frequently upheld as an epitome
of irony. Seinfeld and his sitcom buddies skate over the surface of
real life, avoiding disappointment by evading real commitment; one
imagines these characters, in their post-sitcom years, growing older
as they slowly amuse themselves to death.

Many more examples of this ironic stance could be cited,
especially from the realm of high art (from Warholian soup cans to
elephant dung-bespattered Virgin Marys). But despite my sympathy
for these criticisms of cultural decadence, I find it necessary to
register my dissent, on at least two fronts. First, I believe that using
the word irony to describe the phenomena I've just sketched out is to
abuse a profound and subtle term. And second, I am disturbed by
the number of religious people I've met who have latched onto the
concept of irony as a way of condemning nearly all contemporary
art.

Many of us were told by our high school English teachers that
when a newspaper calls a fatal car wreck "tragic," it is a corruption
of language. The randomness of an accident, however sad, is a far
cry from the classical understanding of tragedy as the fall of a noble
protagonist with a tragic flaw. So it is with irony, one of the central
forms of the imagination. Irony is a capacious term, with an
enormous range of tone and intent, from the tragic, dramatic irony of
Oedipus Rex to the satirical deadpan of Jonathan Swift's *A Modest
Proposal*.

The simplest definition of irony that I've encountered is "the
recognition of a reality different from the masking appearance."
However, the best definition I've encountered was pointed out to me

by the writer Jonathan Raban. It comes from H.W. Fowler's classic work, *Modern English Usage:* "Irony is a form of utterance that postulates a double audience, consisting of one party that hearing shall hear and shall not understand, and another party that, when more is meant than meets the ear, is aware of that more and of the outsider's incomprehension."

The goal of the artist is to enable his or her audience to encounter irony as a moment of recognition, an awareness of the disparity between appearance and reality. Like many of the artist's devices, irony is something of an interactive game, requiring a discerning mind that is willing to sift through the evidence and draw conclusions. When irony is used by the greatest minds, recognition can become revelation, a way of piercing through the ambiguities of daily life to a fleetingly-glimpsed truth.

For this reason, I think that irony is the wrong term for the sort of postmodern self-consciousness we've begun to grow tired of. I've decided that it is better to speak of this cynical habit that puts everything in quotation marks as *bad faith,* because this habit is, ultimately, a form of insincerity and evasion. Irony, on the other hand, is *not* the opposite of sincerity. Used responsibly, irony reminds us of how difficult it is to achieve the transparency of true sincerity. Our *hubris* constantly undermines our quest to discover and communicate truth, which is why irony can put us in our place.

I can understand why some believers think of the pre-modern era of cathedrals as a source of unclouded radiance, whereas our modern, conflicted sensibility lacks that earlier time's plangent faith. And yet, as any glance at the gargoyles on those cathedrals—or the writings of Chaucer and Dante—will show, irony was just as much a part of medieval art as it is today.

Those who are suspicious of irony's indirection might point out that the Devil, speaking through the serpent in Eden, was its first master. In saying that Adam and Eve would not die—and that their eyes would be opened—when they ate the fruit of the tree in the midst of the garden, the serpent was dealing in ironic half-truths. But no sooner had our first parents fallen than the Lord God came down for a stroll in the garden, calling out to his friend Adam, "Where art thou?" Here, in this first game of hide-and-seek, Yahweh demonstrates that he is not to be outdone in the irony department.

To my mind, Jesus is the supreme ironist. It is impossible for me to think of his parables, or the many *koan*-like conundrums he poses to apostles, Pharisees, and gentiles, without sensing his playful use of indirection, that teasing form of testing those who encounter him, that is the essence of irony. When that mysterious figure joins the two apostles on the road to Emmaus, asking them a seemingly innocent question—as Yahweh's call to Adam appeared to be—the ironies begin to pile up. The apostles' lack of faith prevents them from recognizing both the true mission of Jesus and his immediate presence before them. Only when he breaks bread with them—a direct allusion to his sacrificial death and the source of their communion—are their eyes opened. At this very moment, which reverses the false "eye-opening" of Eden, the ironist disappears, bidding us seek him in all the myriad disparities between our blinding pride and his playful love.

The Stock of Available Reality

A few months ago I received a letter which praised *Image* for "adding to the stock of available reality." As I read that phrase, I felt a strange elation—not because it was intended as praise, but because it distilled a great deal of wisdom into very few words. Since the words were set off in quotation marks, I immediately wrote back to ask the source and found it came from a 1935 book review by the eminent critic R.P. Blackmur. The first sentence of that review is worth quoting in full:

> *The art of poetry is amply distinguished from the manufacture of verse by the animating presence in the poetry of a fresh idiom; language so twisted and posed in a form that it not only expresses the matter in hand but adds to the stock of available reality.*

Blackmur here provides as concise a definition of art as one could desire, for his terms apply not just to poetry but to any art form.

True art achieves a "fresh idiom" by twisting and posing its materials in such a way that meaning flashes out and we suddenly learn something new (which is usually something old) about the world. In a sense, Blackmur's definition is close to Coleridge's famous distinction between imagination and fancy. Coleridge likens the imagination to God's act of creation—a fusion of disparate elements into a new whole. Fancy, on the other hand, falls short of the imaginative fusion: it is merely the clever rearranging of fixed and lifeless symbols.

I doubt that Blackmur's words would have struck me so forcefully if they merely provided a capsule definition of art. Indeed, they seem to resonate at a number of different levels. How, for example, does one think about the *stock* of available reality? Does the size of this stock simply accumulate over time, or does it rise and fall through the history of a culture? How much reality is available to us at any given time? If T.S. Eliot was right when he said that "Human kind cannot bear very much reality," then that stock is always in danger of being diminished.

My reflections on these matters came to a head during the days leading up to the awarding of the Oscars in 2000. Watching *American Beauty* sweep all the major awards, I wondered why another worthy contender, *The Sixth Sense,* faired so poorly. Both films were critical successes, featured wonderful acting, and dealt with a serious theme: the paradoxical presence of death in the midst of life.

In the end, I suspect that the success of *American Beauty* stems in part from the film's appeal to some of our culture's most deep-seated myths and fantasies. While there are many telling moments in this black comedy about suburban ennui, the film becomes radically incoherent by its conclusion. Lester Burnham experiences regeneration by quitting his servile job, reverting to his youthful habits of smoking pot and listening to classic rock and roll, and lusting after a high school cheerleader. To be fair, *American Beauty* isn't literally endorsing Lester's return to adolescence: it's too ironic for that. But the moral of the story does seem to echo one of William Blake's "Proverbs of Hell": "The road of excess leads to the palace of

wisdom." At the end we are asked to believe that Lester's pursuit of petty desires leads to a final purgation, so that he is able to recapture his love for his wife and daughter. But as with so many Boomer creations, Lester's final liberation comes without cost—no contrition necessary, and certainly nothing like penance.

Forgiveness and penance are not aspects of reality that many of us willingly embrace. And yet they lie at the heart of writer-director M. Night Shyamalan's enormously popular film *The Sixth Sense*. It is impossible to explain the success of this movie merely on the basis of a surprise ending or some spooky scenes or even the remarkable acting of young Haley Joel Osment, playing the visionary child, Cole

Sear. What draws people to this film is the deeper mystery—the true surprise—the story reveals: that the dead are not out to scare us silly, but to beg us for help: forgiveness, understanding, and compassion.

In *The Sixth Sense* adults think they see the world clearly, but pride blinds them; they go about their business without fear, believing what they want to believe. The boy, on the other hand, has no blinders, no defense mechanisms: he sees all the pain and confusion in the world, but because he doesn't understand it, he is filled with fear. In the spiritual alchemy of this story, the child helps the man to see, and only then can the man help the child to set aside fear and gain the courage of compassion. Together they draw near to a mystery that the church tried to comprehend in the idea of Purgatory. And so an ancient religious theme is given a "fresh idiom."

The Sixth Sense is a work of art that makes available—or bearable, to use Eliot's term—layers of reality that most of us treat with varying levels of denial. Shyamalan's film, so redolent of his Catholic and Episcopal education in the Philadelphia area, is nevertheless representative of a wider revival of religious vision in contemporary literature and art. *Image* has sought not only to reflect this revival but also to foster it. The stocks are being replenished for those with eyes to see and ears to hear.

Transfiguration

O F all the passages in the Bible that relate to beauty as a window onto the divine, the most neglected, and most important, is the story known as the Transfiguration. On the surface, nothing about this episode speaks directly about art, beauty, or the imagination. But placed in the right context, one can see in this passage a spiritual aesthetic. I have found such a context in the writings of the late Hans Urs von Balthasar, arguably the greatest Catholic theologian of the twentieth century. Von Balthasar believed that the word "glory" in the Bible is synonymous with the beauty of God. Of the three transcendental attributes of God—truth, goodness, and beauty—von Balthasar held that beauty is the least obscured by our fallen nature, and thus provides us with the clearest path to the Beatific Vision.

According to von Balthasar, the essential starting point for the human encounter with the divine is a moment of aesthetic perception, that glimpse of radiance, mystery, and meaning we see in a work of art or in the natural world.

In the context of von Balthasar's theology, the seemingly straightforward story of the Transfiguration takes on new twists; like a parable, it is full of paradox and implicit challenges to our moral and spiritual inertia. Jesus takes Peter, James, and John up to the mountain to pray. There his countenance is altered and his garments shine with a blinding light. At his side appear Moses and Elijah. Luke's gospel continues the story:

> But Peter and they that were with him were heavy with sleep: and when they were awake, they saw his glory, and the two men that stood with him. And it came to pass, as they departed from him, Peter said unto Jesus, Master, it is good for us to be here: and let us make three tabernacles; one for thee, and one for Moses, and one for Elias [Elijah]: not knowing what he said. While he thus spake, there came a cloud, and overshadowed them: and they feared as they entered into the cloud. And there came a voice out of the cloud, saying, This is my beloved Son: hear him. And when the voice was past, Jesus was found alone.

The Transfiguration hearkens back to Moses' own encounter with the divine in the form of the burning bush, and it looks forward to the mysterious post-Resurrection body of Jesus. In each instance, glory is experienced as a transformation that does not consume or destroy what is being transformed. The ordinary becomes extraordinary without becoming something wholly other.

At this point, it's easy to see why the narrative offers numerous analogies to art and beauty. Thomas Aquinas defined beauty as the splendor of form, the flash of radiance that is at once intensely pleasurable and filled with meaning. In the Transfiguration, the burning light that once appeared to Moses in the bush now pulses from Jesus himself, revealing him as the God-man, the icon of the Father. Beauty and meaning embrace.

Of course, it's when we turn to the disciples and their reactions that the story begins to take on elements of both comedy and pathos. Heavy with sleep, their senses dulled, the disciples are not prepared for this sudden blast of cosmic radiation. Peter, the patron saint of all those who make the right mistakes, tries to capture and hold on to this manifestation of divine presence, not knowing that we cannot contain such mystery, that to do so leads only to distortion and arrogant system-building. This moment offers Luke the opportunity to write one of the drollest lines in the Bible, as he describes Peter as having spoken, "not knowing what he said."

As if to emphasize the paradoxical tension between presence and absence, what is understood and what is only seen through a glass darkly, a cloud descends on the mountain. Out of this "cloud of unknowing" (to borrow the title of a medieval mystical treatise), meaning emerges as something underwritten only by God's own voice and authority. So it must always be: beauty comes and goes in the blink of an eye, sovereign but elusive. In much the same way, after the Resurrection, Jesus will appear—and disappear—leaving his disciples reeling, but perhaps not quite as sleepy as they once were.

Some of the early Church fathers held that in the Transfiguration it was the disciples who changed, not Christ. Because their perception grew sharper, they were able to behold Christ as he truly is.

At its best, art transfigures the world around us for a brief time, strives to let the radiance of truth, goodness, and beauty flash out for an instant. Art wakes us up, trains our perceptions, and reminds us that when we try to build rigid structures around presence we inevitably lose what we attempt to keep. The purpose of art is not to strand us in an alternate world, but to return us to the realm of the ordinary, only with new eyes. After the light had dimmed and the cloud had dispersed, the disciples found Jesus alone. Seeing their bewilderment, he must have had compassion for them. He must also have known that, though the disciples were temporarily blinded by the light, an image had been imprinted on their hearts that would never be erased.

Playing With God

THERE are times, I must confess, when I find it difficult to explain what kind of glue holds together the various and disparate projects I've worked on over the years. Of course, I know it's foolish to try to impose an artificial unity on one's works and days, but there are moments when I'm nagged by a recurring dichotomy. It's like an old bone injury that flares up when the barometer changes. Perhaps that metaphor concedes too much, because I believe that there is an inner consistency in my work. I am always distressed when someone who appreciates one project I'm involved in has no time for another.

Perhaps the most persistent dichotomy I've encountered lies on the divide between the books that my wife Suzanne and I have written on developing the moral and spiritual dimensions of a child's heart and the publishing of *Image*. There are those who applaud our efforts in the areas of character education and the spirituality of children who cannot understand why we would publish a journal that occasionally features edgy art, paintings of nude bodies, four-letter words, and so on. Undoubtedly there are those who have the opposite problem; they may wonder, for example, why *Image* frequently carries interviews with, and essays by, writers of "children's literature" (such as the interview in issue #28 with Donna Jo Napoli, Eileen and Jerry Spinelli).

What I find curious about these viewpoints is not merely that they reflect age-old generation gaps, or the perennial debate between art and morality, but that they seem to grow out of a diminished understanding of childhood. The conservatives who have spearheaded the "back to the virtues" movement are certainly providing a much-needed corrective to liberal notions about each child being free to choose his or her own values. But alas, many champions of morality seem to think that the good, the true, and the beautiful are monolithic entities that can simply be dumped into children's heads with the right selection of didactic tales. If that were so, what need would we have of either art or morality in the first place? Good and evil don't exist as Platonic ideas, but are, more often than not, entangled in the ambiguities of everyday life. That's why so much of the best children's literature is about the terrifying and dramatic quest on the part of the hero to sort out appearance from reality, to follow the trail of breadcrumbs through the dense and menacing forest back to the safety and security of home.

Censors on both left and right who have criticized the violence and harshness of the classic fairy tales talk in terms of preserving the innocence and wonder of children. But deep down I believe that what these censors fear is the play of imagination itself, the capacity that enables us to suspend disbelief—and moral judgment—for a time in order to sort reality out from appearance. To the modern puritan, imagination is a form of idle play that refuses to get on with the urgent work of moral and political character formation. But I would contend that the opposite is true: only when we play can we find the inner space needed to allow our deepest intuitions about the world to inform our reason.

Josef Pieper's classic book *Leisure: The Basis of Culture,* while not about children per se, provides some illumination here. In it he argues that philosophy and theology are grounded in leisure, which offers a restorative retreat from the driving purposefulness of work. He cites with approval Thomas Aquinas's belief that contemplation, the highest act of the human spirit, is akin to play. Later in the book, Pieper writes brilliantly about the idea of wonder itself, that capacity shared by children and philosophers alike. Pieper claims that wonder should not be sentimentalized into something saccharin and static. Rather, "wonder acts upon a man like a shock, he is 'moved' and 'shaken,' and in the dislocation that succeeds all that he had taken for granted as being natural or self-evident loses its compact solidity and obviousness; he is literally dislocated and no longer knows where he is." According to Pieper, to wonder is "not to know fully." This condition is not doubt but the awareness that truth is hidden, shrouded in mystery. Wonder may involve a state of not-knowing, but it does not end there; it is, Pieper insists, a process, an experience of being "on the way" toward the meaning at the heart of mystery.

In our book, *Circle of Grace: Praying with—and for—Your Children,* we also stress the relationship between prayer and play. We mean no sacrilege by it. To say that prayer and the imagination are closely related is not to claim that prayer is merely speaking into the void. On the contrary, the words and rituals of prayer give us the space we need so that we can sound the depths of the mystery in which God is cloaked. If we approach prayer (or art or life) with the grim drivenness of the one-dimensional moralist, we will end in

spiritual claustrophobia. Play can be solemn as well as joyful, which is a reminder that neither prayer nor art should exclude the harsh, violent, or ambiguous realities that confront us every day. In our experience, children can withstand the shock and dislocation that wonder entails. Indeed, they need such multi-dimensional wonder as much as they need food and drink, light and love. And so I venture to hope that *Image* and our books about children are merely different ways of trying to become like children playing in the fields of the Lord.

Fugitive Energies

IN his essay, "How the West Lost Its Story," theologian Robert W. Jenson argues that we postmoderns no longer inhabit what he calls a "narratable world." The heart of Western civilization, he notes, has been the biblical story, which posited a coherent, dramatic narrative—a world that had a beginning, middle, and at least a vision of an end. (The novelist Walker Percy used to say that the story he believed in could be put in four words: "God Jews Jesus Church.")

Jenson goes on to say that modernity, which replaced the biblical narrative with reason, tried to cling to the idea of a world that could be understood as a story. But without belief in a divine storyteller, Jenson says, the modernist project was doomed to fail. Which is why, he concludes, the postmodern world has no story. He cites Surrealism and the theater of the absurd as the first waves of postmodern art: arrangements of objects that don't have a proper relationship to one another, sequences of words and events with "no turning points or denouement."

Like all strong theories, Jenson's argument sheds a great deal of light on a vast historical canvas. As an overview of Western history, there's much to commend in it. But big theories have a way of riding roughshod over recalcitrant facts. For example, while one might grant Jenson that Surrealism and absurdist theater reflect a world whose intelligibility is in question, it *is* possible to uncover buried narratives in the paintings of René Magritte and the plays of Samuel Beckett (the two artists he cites as representative postmodernists). But beyond debating Jenson's interpretation of modern artists and their styles, there is another pesky reality, which is that stories with beginnings, middles, and ends continue to be told (though not always in that order). As a culture we may lack a shared, unifying story, but I don't believe that the old, old story has gone away.

What interests me are the ways in which the biblical story continues to be told, even in the strangest of guises. Like the Tar Baby that Brer Fox sets out in the road for Brer Rabbit to encounter, the story can be punched, shattered, inverted, buried, and even trivialized, and like ol' Tar Baby it tends to stick to those who touch it, and never more fiercely than to those who seek to overcome it.

When James Joyce attempts, in *The Portrait of the Artist as a Young Man,* to put forward the artist as the high priest of a secular age, the writing depends on our making an analogy with the biblical understanding of priesthood; there is no way to take the Jesuit education out of Joyce without making nonsense of his vision. Beckett may present us with a world bereft of divine presence, but try comprehending Godot without God.

Popular culture offers examples galore of biblical transmutations. At a recent conference I attended, the cultural historian John T. Fisher spoke of pop culture as the locus where we might spot the "fugitive energies" of the gospel. Among his examples were Andy Warhol's celebrity silk screens, works that are widely derided but which no less a critic than Richard Rodriguez admires as a vestige of Warhol's childhood Catholicism. Warhol, Rodriguez writes, had an incarnational perspective. He saw "everything in the world redeemed. 'Everyone will be famous for fifteen minutes,' Andy Warhol famously said. Most people only hear the tail end of his dictum, the 'fifteen minutes,' but Andy Warhol said, 'Everyone will be famous.'" Fisher also singled out the films of Kevin Smith, including *Clerks.* According to Fisher: "Smith wants us to see how much Catholic energy has been invested in the materials of everyday life and how futile it is to seek the boundaries of the sacred and the profane. The clerks (clerics) at the Quick Stop engage in some of the most fervent verbal disputation this side of neo-scholasticism, as distinctions between nature and grace are rerouted into a virtuoso debate over the respective merits of *The Return of the Jedi* and *The Empire Strikes Back.*"

There is much to bemoan about the state of our culture, and in a different mood I might complain about the dethronement of the biblical story and the fragmented world we inhabit. But isn't our consolation that we must be on the lookout for the way the fugitive energies inherent in the "God Jews Jesus Church" story have spread out, like seeds in the wind, to inhabit countless stories and to surprise and bless us from a host of unlikely destinations?

In Cormac McCarthy's masterpiece, *The Crossing,* an old storyteller tries to explain his task to a young man:

The task of the narrator is not an easy one, he said. He appears to be required to choose his tale from among the many that are possible. But of course that is not the case. The case is rather to make many of the one. Always the teller must be at pains to devise against his listener's claim—perhaps spoken, perhaps not—that he has heard the tale before. He sets forth the categories into which the listener will wish to fit the narrative as he hears it. But he understands that the narrative is itself in fact no category but is rather the category of all categories for there is nothing which falls outside its purview. All is telling.

There is but one story to tell. It is a story ever ancient, ever new— a story that takes an infinite number of forms. It cannot be contained, but leaps from the sacred to the profane and back again. It is told and retold, becoming tragedy, comedy, fairy tale, farce. It's our Tar Baby.

The Form of Faith

WHEN, about a year ago, I saw the cover of a special arts issue of *Re:generation*, a journal I generally admire, I bristled. The cover headline read "Artists, Come Home!" and the illustration included a mock "personal" ad calling on artists to return to the church. What struck me as wrong, I think, was the implication that artists were inherently wayward folk, and that the journal was somehow in a position to call these prodigal children home. In a letter to the editor, I pointed out that the contents of that issue contradicted the cover, since the artists featured were all deeply ensconced in churches and communities. Moreover, I said, the idea of the artist as someone likely to stray from the fold reinforced a deep American prejudice, fueled by our religious history, that those who live by their imaginations are predisposed to wantonness of various sorts. That prejudice not only does a disservice to the many artists who live within church communities (men and women who frequently feel unappreciated by their brothers and sisters), but also sends a message to those on the outside, and not a terribly attractive one.

But to prove that I'm not troubled by the hobgoblin of foolish consistency, I'd like to say a word about those writers and artists who do find themselves estranged from communities of faith. It isn't hard to empathize with creative people who feel profound ambivalence about organized religion. Any form of organization is going to exert a pressure toward conventional thinking and expression that will run afoul of the artist's passion to "make it new." Like families, churches can become dysfunctional and inflict wounds down to the bone of one's psyche. (Anyone who studies art in any detail is also aware of the mysterious relationship between the traumas that

religious groups can cause and the very budding and flowering of imagination in response to such pain.)

There are, however, countervailing pressures on the artist, pressures that lead in the direction of community, rather than away from it. Take, for example, the close connection between artistic vision and prophetic insight. Artists have often rightly considered their role in prophetic terms. But the prophet is never completely independent of community. In ancient Israel, prophets actually held an office; though they were more free to speak their minds than others, they were not autonomous. As I've argued before, the office of prophet was not the same as that of priest or king, and the prophet had no right to arrogate those roles to himself. The tendency of a few artists to assume these other roles has been with us at least since the Romantic era, but it has done very little to contribute to the creation of enduring works of imagination.

An even more compelling argument goes to the heart of the creative act. All art involves an intimate union between form and content. So intimate is this unity that it would be wrong to describe the relationship merely by saying that form is like a vessel that contains content, as a bowl might contain milk. It is natural to speak of form as something exterior and content as something interior, but it is also misleading. We may speak of the theme of a work of art but we should never do so as if the theme is something that can be detached from the work's form. Form is mediation: it makes something intangible known to us—in and through tangible words, gestures, materials.

Now apply all this to faith. For the Jew, the content of belief, the existence of the Maker and Lord of the universe, is mediated through the form of the covenant, a relationship between the Lord and the chosen people. To be sure, there are various denominations within Judaism, but they do not divide the fundamental unity of the Jewish people. In Christianity, the content—the Gospel of salvation through Christ—is mediated through the form of the church. The perennial temptation for Christians is to believe that the message can be detached from the community of believers in that message. But the content of faith is precisely that we are members of one body, that Christ is made manifest in our coming together in faith.

The church, it is said, is a human institution, and a thoroughly fallible one at that. True, but as every artist ought to know, all our forms are imperfect—they are broken vessels. To acknowledge that brokenness is not to invalidate the need to create and strive perpetually to perfect those forms. The wonder of art, and of faith, is that we can still receive grace through the cracks in those vessels. As Leonard Cohen put it: "There are cracks, cracks, in everything, that's how the light gets in."

In describing his writing process, C.S. Lewis spoke of beginning with a ferment of "mental pictures" colliding in his imagination. "This ferment leads to nothing unless it is accompanied with the longing for a Form," he concludes. All of us have been vouchsafed mental pictures of transcendent truth, but we need to find a form to give them coherence and meaning. In that sense, the church is not only form, but truly our home. Which brings me back to that cover headline. Yes, artists should come home, but no one can issue that call to anyone else from a safe, ensconced position inside that home. For we are all wayward, and only arrive home by daily seeking it out—preferably in the company of one another.

Please Touch

HAVING grown up in what I would call a rather Waspy milieu in New York's Upper East Side, my youthful aesthetic sensibility was, to some extent, predetermined. My mother took me to see the classics of art history at the Metropolitan, but she also took me to the Museum of Modern Art and the Guggenheim. I was surrounded by the austere simplicity of High Modernism; that slow ascending spiral of Frank Lloyd Wright's Guggenheim was as much a part of my mental landscape as it was the cityscape of my neighborhood.

In those childhood years, we attended a Christian Science church, so my religious aesthetic was similarly shaped by a sort of minimalist neoclassicism. When we switched to the Congregational Church in my adolescence, I could detect no real change in architecture and only a modest expansion of liturgical possibilities.

Even in my college years, when I had become an Episcopalian and an ardent believer in the centrality of sign and sacrament for the life of faith, I tended to like the spareness of stone cathedrals, with their gray verticality. It was only when I went to a cathedral in England that I learned that medieval stone churches were painted in vivid colors, that they were, in fact, a riot of sensory stimulation. This was a blow, but it made me realize that I had treated Gothic stone more as a proto-modernist achievement than the sensual, organic thing it really was. So I began to notice other architectural styles, including the Baroque, and to actually pay attention to statuary, the depiction of saints, angels, and gargoyles.

My aesthetic was beginning to yield, and with it my faith. When I was a child, my spirituality, echoing the architecture around me, seemed to consist of ethical simplicity, the recollection of ancient but enduring ideas—something to be experienced in the head, rather than the heart. Perhaps one of the legacies of my early immersion in Christian Science was a feeling that the human body was something of an embarrassment, if not a prison. But I wasn't satisfied with this. I didn't want to be a ghost in my own flesh.

So began a journey that eventually led me into the Roman Catholic church. Not surprisingly, the Virgin Mary did not play a large role in my religious search. I found Marian kitsch—the gaudy popular Catholic representations of Mary, in plastic and plaster—so alien and off-putting that I wondered if I could ever become a co-religionist with the people who made and venerated such things. Deep cultural programming told me that the folks who came up to these figures—leaving flowers at their feet, hanging rosaries on the outstretched hand of the Christ child, touching the base of the elevated statues so that the paint rubbed off the toes of the Virgin—were more like primitive pantheists than civilized believers.

It took years for me to realize that what kept me away from Mary was not merely a disdain for popular Catholic devotion, but my own abstracted and overly cerebral faith. A slowly developing hunger for the sacraments—for the grace of God to be not merely understood or even felt, but actually *touched,* in the common stuff of life, including bread, wine, water, and oil—eventually brought me closer to Mary. For she was the human vessel whose womb and breasts and arms and tear ducts were the necessary conduits through which the Son of God became the Son of Man. I no longer felt satisfied thinking about God; I needed to feel his touch on my tongue.

And then I looked again at all those representations of Mary, from hideously bejeweled plastic dolls to numinously beautiful alabaster statues, and I could see one message conveyed over and over again. As Our Lady holds the child, simultaneously protecting him and presenting him to the world that would crucify him, she seems to say to us: Please Touch.

Representations of Mary seem to revel in paradox: as Virgin she is untouched, but as Mother she is constantly touching others. In all those paintings of the Annunciation, Mary is depicted as praying or reading at the moment she receives the message from Gabriel, but even in contemplation her body language is eloquent—she recoils and assents in one complicated gesture. At the foot of the cross she receives her son into her arms once more. As refuge of sinners, she spreads her mantle around gathered humanity, protecting and consoling.

This came home to me once when I was praying in El Santuario de Chimayo, the New Mexican chapel that has become known as the Lourdes of America. Chimayo is the place where the Virgin appeared to a local farmer and answered his prayer by blessing the barren earth and making it fecund. This, too, is about touch, for the earth is the skin of the world.

As I was praying and daydreaming a Hispanic woman came toward the front of the chapel. She paid no attention to the magnificent nineteenth-century painted reredos in the Spanish colonial style, but approached a small, mass-produced plaster statue of the Virgin. Wracked by sobs and streaming tears, the woman was inconsolable. It was impossible to tell what she mourned. But over the next ten minutes she drew close to the statue and touched it with her outstretched fingertips, with a strange combination of reticence and compulsion. She would touch and then withdraw a number of times in an agonized dance that somehow seemed to me at that moment to be steps taken from the choreography of heaven. Eventually a friend guided her out of the sanctuary. I couldn't be sure but I thought that she had experienced some small measure of consolation, that some exchange had taken place in that dance, that hesitant, confident touching of the Mother.

Falling Towers

IN the final section of *The Waste Land,* T.S. Eliot strives to integrate two dimensions of the poem that have been running on parallel tracks: the snapshots of inner, psychic alienation and the critique of a decadent social order. Eliot lists a series of cities: "Jerusalem Athens Alexandria / Vienna London." The list plots out the course of Western civilization, from its origins in classical and biblical cultures to its modern European efflorescence. As with so much of the poem, Eliot is being cryptic, particularly in his choice of the two modern cities. One can understand London: the cradle of democracy and the rule of law. But Vienna? Is there a hint in that choice of a civilization gone to seed, a place of elegance and opulence, yes, but a falling off from the human search for the order of the soul and the order of the commonwealth? And does London, by its place on the sequence, also exist on the downward slope of cultural history?

The list of cities is preceded by the two-word line: "Falling towers." While there may be no specific textual allusion here, the reader's mind reaches out for connections: to the Tower of Babel, certainly, with its theme of human pride and overreaching; perhaps also the story Jesus tells about the tower of Siloam, which collapses without warning and kills innocent people, a reminder of our mortality and a spur for all of us to be prepared for death.

If Eliot were writing today, he would surely have to add New York to his list. The urban trajectory that the Eurocentric Eliot traced was already questionable in 1922, but within a couple decades it became obsolete, as the United States emerged as sole proprietor of "the American century." Now we all have a mental videotape, perpetually looping back on itself, of our own falling towers. Now, in the aftermath of the September 11, 2001 terrorist attacks, we are all New Yorkers.

It is right to mourn our lost and praise our heroes. As we seek to apprehend the perpetrators and take measures to prevent future attacks, things get more complicated. There are those who, out of religious or ethical conviction, condemn the use of force in the campaign against terror. The argument has merit, but for me it is not the lynchpin issue. What worries me more is that Americans will fail, once again, to learn the deepest lessons of this most teachable of moments. There are two related modes of thought that Americans have always avoided—historical consciousness and the tragic sense of life.

Our national origins are inextricably bound up with the idea of American exceptionalism, the vision of a nation as *novus ordo seclorum,* a new order of the ages. The shining city on a hill is a city out of time, unburdened by the weight of history. Its towers never fall. And so its language is based on triumph; it is the perpetual underdog/self-made man achieving victory against enemies who are mired in the past. Prosperity is the measure of its success. (In the typical thriller, the rugged American individualist, armed with the latest technology, always defeats a villain who comes from a culture that may have wonderful architecture and customs, but who is weighed down by way too much historical baggage.)

On this score, the dominant strains both of American Christianity and what the political scientists call "civil religion" are at one.

In the rhetoric of recent days, several *faux pas* in our choice of language have threatened to deconstruct the tidy compartmental-izing of good vs. evil and freedom vs. tyranny. Take, for example, the President's comment that in fighting terrorism we had launched a "crusade." Then there was "Infinite Justice," the original name for the military operation in Afghanistan. In both cases, the dark side of Western progressivism—the hubris of cultural imperialism—briefly reared its head. For millions of people on this planet, the word *crusade* is freighted with historical meaning and infinite justice is an attribute of God alone.

No act of evil, however heinous, can be completely wrenched from its cultural and psychic context: that is the lesson of historical consciousness. To condemn the act without exploring the context is a form of denial, not moral strength. That our actions must always arise out of mixed motives and bring about evil as well as good: that is the teaching of the tragic sense of life.

T.S. Eliot understood this by the time he wrote *Four Quartets.* Though he had embraced Christian faith and the Western tradition, Eliot had come to believe that the very essence of that tradition was its awareness of the ambiguity of human actions. In *Four Quartets,*

most of which was written during the Second World War, Eliot
provided solace for a generation, but he did so by stressing the need
for humility, not triumphalistic national pride. In these lines he
explored the paradox that action and suffering are inextricably
linked. "Every phrase and every sentence is an end and a beginning,
/ Every poem an epitaph. And any action / is a step to the block,
down the sea's throat / Or to an illegible stone...."

In the aftermath of September 11, some have called for an end to
irony. Others have stressed our need for comedy. But the urgent need
of the moment is a deeper embrace of tragedy. America's greatest
Christian writers, from Hawthorne to Eliot, O'Connor, and Percy,

have been accused of
turning their backs on our
national genius in favor of a
dark European vision. But in
their historical sensibility
and their belief that grace is
most often found through
suffering, these writers
represent the best in the
American tradition. In this
time of grief and anger,
these writers—the real
underdogs of American literary culture—offer us the surest
guidance to prudent action and to healing.

A Sacrifice of Praise

AT the heart of every well-made work of art—no matter how dark or disturbing it may be—is an act of praise. In Mark Jarman's review of Elaine Scarry's *On Beauty and Being Just* in issue #33 of *Image* he recounts Scarry's contention that beauty tends to call forth, or beget, more beauty. The beauty of a face, sunset, vase, or brushstroke evokes in the viewer an answering gesture: the desire to describe or reproduce that beauty in some fashion. For the artist, this will involve making a sketch, writing a lyric, choreographing a dance. In that responsive gesture is the essence of praise. Praise is a form of giving back, a way of doing justice by rendering to the world what it is due. At its best, praise has an ontological dimension—a reveling in what-is, a blessing of being itself.

Like anything human, praise seems at once natural and unnatural. When we find ourselves in the grip of suffering and insecurity praise is not the first thing to leap to our lips. In one of his finest poems, "Psalm Against Psalms," Andrew Hudgins confesses that he finds praise the most difficult form of prayer. Comparing himself with the prophets—poets who transformed tragedy and suffering into praise—Hudgins can only feel that he comes up short.

> Isaiah ate the blood-red ember.
> Ezekiel ate the dung. It went in fire
> and came out praise. It went in shit
> and came out praise from his mouth. And this
> is where I stick. I pray: thank, ask,
> confess. But praise—dear God!—it clings
> like something dirty on my tongue . . . .

Hudgins is describing what another prophet, Jeremiah, called "a sacrifice of praise." When it comes to sacrificing ourselves, we're all unwilling victims.

In *The Brothers Karamazov,* the tortured, alienated Ivan tells Alyosha that he cannot accept this world—a world in which children can suffer and die—that he wants to give back his ticket. And yet, he admits that he still loves life. "Though I may not believe in the order of the universe, yet I love the sticky little leaves as they open in spring." Ivan goes on to tell the story of the Grand Inquisitor, in which Jesus, after returning in the flesh to Spain, is arrested and interrogated. The Inquisitor's message, of course, is that of Ivan: human beings do not want, and cannot bear, the freedom that Christ came to bring; they prefer slavery to freedom and illusion to reality, the Inquisitor says to Jesus, who remains silent throughout the interrogation and, at the very end, rises and kisses his adversary on the lips. Alyosha, who gets up to kiss Ivan, tells his brother that his story is actually in praise of Christ. Those sticky leaves may yet save Ivan from despair.

Today, of course, plenty of unrepentant Ivans are making art that reflects a rejection of the world. So much of the art and literature of our time seems to be cabined, cribbed, and confined within the artist's ego, where the only praise solicited is praise of the artist. Most people have an intuitive measuring stick by which to gauge the art they encounter. Art that is characterized by metaphysical stinginess may preoccupy our minds for a time, but it ultimately fails to engage our hearts.

On the other side of the cultural divide is the sprawling contemporary Christian piety industry, which specializes in praise, which must always be accompanied by sweat and swelling chords. But here too something rings false. Here the praise, while ostensibly offered to God above, seems stubbornly earth-bound, equated more with the emotional agitation of the individual than the sticky-leaves-and-suffering-children messiness of this world. In the Bible, praise broadens out to encompass the scary along with the sweet. Psalm 148 envisions praise bursting forth from the unlikeliest of places: "Praise the LORD from the earth, you sea monsters and all deeps, fire and hail, snow and frost, stormy wind fulfilling his command!" That praise seems capable of bursting from the humblest elements of the created order is a constant theme in the Bible. St. Paul gives this a cosmic twist when he says that "We know that the whole creation has been groaning in travail together until now." Coming from an alleged misogynist, there is something stunning and potent about St. Paul's metaphor of a woman in labor. In that image, suffering and hope embrace; desire and pain bear fruit.

In a recent essay Belden C. Lane argues that another much-abused religious leader, John Calvin, saw a direct relationship between praise and desire. Lane writes: "Praise, for Calvin, is a performative utterance. It springs from an inner disposition of intense desire, while at the same time possessing a capacity to influence, by its longing, the object of its love. The act of praising has a double effect—subjectively stirring desire in the one who celebrates and objectively evoking (making present and efficacious) what is celebrated."

And so it is perhaps not a stretch to say that praise is also eschatological, because it presses on toward the end and consummation of things. When I am absorbed in a great work of art—say, a Shakespeare play—I have a sense, hard to pin down but just below the surface of my consciousness, that all the complications of plot and image, surface and depth, comedy and tragedy, will in the end give way to a hymn of praise.

When the players come out after the curtain falls, we applaud not only their skill and that of the playwright, but the larger cosmic stage on which we are privileged to act. "Hurrah for Karamazov," the children say at the end of Dostoevsky's novel, praising not only Alyosha, but the sticky leaves and the whole of our groaning and travailing creation.

The Painter of Lite™

LAST night, after the kids' final day of school and a hard slog at work, our family sat down to watch *Jurassic Park III*, the kind of movie we call E.T. ("entertaining trash"). Like most Hollywood sequels the film is full of recycled scenes—mainly dinosaurs energetically masticating just about any piece of flesh that comes their way—but one episode was particularly memorable. During a harrowing encounter with yet another super-sized reptile, one of the terrorized human beings manages to place a call on a satellite telephone. The call is answered by a three year-old in a suburban American home, but instead of going to give the phone to his mom, he gets distracted by the television, which is showing the children's program featuring Barney the cuddly purple T. Rex. While the bloodcurdling sounds of human screams and dinosaur roars come out of the phone, the boy is transfixed by the sight of Barney, who is galumphing about the TV screen to the rhythms of a happy song.

Reflecting on the pleasure I took from that scene, I decided that it was a salutary warning about the difficulty of writing about sentimentality and popular culture. The sheer fun of beating up on artistic kitsch is hard for some of us to resist, and in my title I have succumbed to temptation. The reference, for those who have been living in a different galaxy, is to the painter and marketing genius Thomas Kinkade, who styles himself The Painter of Light™. Kinkade's saccharin, soft-focus paintings of Cotswoldy cottages, glowing gardens, misty lighthouses, and quaint villages have been reproduced over ten million times, and now adorn not only people's walls, but also La-Z-Boy recliners, screen savers, and coffee mugs all over the world. But Kinkade isn't satisfied with his role as artist: he has invested his work with the aura of patriotism and the intentional language of a Christian missionary. When you buy one of his works, whether it is a mug or one of the mass-produced prints that are then "highlighted" by "trained master highlighters," Kinkade wants you to believe that you are furthering the work of the Kingdom.

The critics, on the other hand, are not impressed. They have called Kinkade "a male Martha Stewart" and dubbed his work "art as a Happy Meal," "cultural Prozac," and the painterly equivalent to Beanie Babies.

The problem with comments like these is that they run the risk of backfiring, amounting to little more than a bloodsport of the cultural elite. After all, in America there is an ingrained populism which holds that ten million people can't be wrong. And it is hard to argue with a number that large; Kinkade has connected with some deep human need.

However, it would be a mistake to reduce the discussion of sentimentality to a conflict between earnest populists and alienated elites. There have been popular artists, like Shakespeare and Michelangelo, who never seemed to indulge in sentimentality, while some sophisticated artists, such as Raphael and Dickens, can't be thought of apart from it.

In the eighteenth century, idealist moral philosophers used the word sentimental to express a sense of refinement and sensitivity. The idealists were Enlightenment figures who believed in the innate goodness of man; they felt that the cultivation of emotion allowed that goodness to gain greater social force. Nineteenth-century novelists like Dickens and Thackeray were deeply influenced by this way of thinking, but within fifty years of its coining, the word was being held up to ridicule.

The word sentimentality is now a term of opprobrium, but it is notoriously hard to define. Of course, that hasn't prevented it from being the source of a few witty epigrams. The Zen scholar R. H. Blyth once noted: "We are being sentimental when we give to a thing more tenderness than God gives to it." That's good, but as usual Oscar Wilde hits closer to the mark: "a sentimentalist is one who desires to have the luxury of an emotion without paying for it."

Some thinkers have tried to characterize certain emotions as inherently sentimental, but I am convinced by Mark Jefferson, who argues in a brilliant essay, "What's Wrong with Sentimentality?," that the phenomenon resides not so much in the emotion itself as in the disjuncture between emotion and object. The heart of the problem is that of a misrepresentation of the world in order to indulge certain emotional states. For Jefferson, sentimentality is the product of moral choice. Our vision of the world is shaped by many small choices, which can include a tendency to ascribe "qualities of innocence" to certain objects. Sentimentality, he concludes, ascribes "sweetness, dearness, littleness, blamelessness, and vulnerability" to a select group of things.

Sentimentality, Jefferson admits, can be harmless. A penchant for Hallmark cards and posters of kittens playing with balls of yarn is not in itself a mortal sin. But when the misrepresentation of the world takes on a particular consistency and brittleness, darker consequences are possible. "The unlikely creature and moral carica-ture that is someone unambiguously worthy of sympathetic response has its natural counterpart in a moral caricature of something unambiguously worthy of hatred," Jefferson concludes.

Which is why some observers have noted a relationship between sentimentality and brutality. The example that is usually trotted out here is that of the Nazi doctors, men who could shed tears over a string quartet one moment and then butcher a human being the next. It's a compelling story, but I would contend that it is such an extreme example as to do more to blind us to the quotidian dangers of sentimentality than to enlighten us. To the extent that anything is considered innocent—whether it be a race, nation, class, ethnic group, religion, or what have you—it is held up as something pure, something that can only be tainted or displaced by outside influences. When we are too tender about something we can easily become too violent in seeking to defend or preserve it.

To return to my earlier example, what scares me about Thomas Kinkade is not so much the treacly emotion he seeks to evoke or his inveterate prettifying of nature, but the political subtext underlying his iconography. The only folk who could ever have inhabited his cottages and lighthouses are prosperous white folk. Nearly all of his paintings are of a world circa 1800-1914, with perhaps a small percentage depicting a world between 1914 and 1960. He likes to say that he is a painter of "memories and traditions," but he is highly selective in what he chooses to remember, and that choice bears an unnerving resemblance to a world that is comfortingly pre-modern and Anglo-Saxon in composition. The views of these homes are always from the outside looking in, the point of view as a yearning gaze at windows glowing with light and wisps of smoke rising from chimneys. Here Kinkade demonstrates his genius, because he leaves us free to imagine the idealized world within.

The essence of Kinkade's sentimentality is the packaging of nostalgia. It's an oxymoronic idea, but it has become a major part of our cultural life, as Florence King has noted: "True nostalgia is an ephemeral composition of disjointed memories...but American-style nostalgia is about as ephemeral as copyrighted déjà vu."

Kinkade's patriotism and his attacks on the horrors of artistic modernism are standard-issue conservative notions. When it comes to theology, however, he is a little more original. The majority of his expressions of faith are fairly conventional, solidly within the evangelical mold, but his theological defense of the world depicted in his paintings is that "I like to portray a world without the Fall." I have yet to encounter any evidence that Kinkade cites scriptural or other warrant for this modus operandi. The Bible, as a narrative, seems fairly explicit about there being a Before and an After. Moreover, Christ's message was not to pretend the world isn't fallen but to take up our crosses and follow him through suffering and sacrifice. To create a body of work illustrating a world without the Fall is, for a Christian, to render Christ superfluous.

The more I've thought about it, the more it seems to me that Jesus took every opportunity he could to counter sentimentality. At just about every juncture when those around him are tempted to rely upon sentiment, he brings them up short. To the announcement that his mother and brothers have arrived at the edge of the crowd—a Hallmark moment if ever there was one—he replies that only his disciples are his mother and brothers. And the one recorded instance when Jesus weeps takes place after he has deliberately delayed coming to see the dying Lazarus. In John's recounting of the story, Jesus is clearly moved by the suffering of the man's family, and perhaps his awareness of this death and resurrection as proleptic of his own passion. But whatever emotions he was feeling—grief, pity, regret—they were inexorably shaped by the reality of the Fall.

Kinkade's apologetic seems to fit the definition of sentimentality as the "misrepresentation of the world in order to indulge certain emotional states." That he is tapping into a deep human need seems unquestionable. But the response that he and many other purveyors of subcultural religious kitsch provide to that need is both inadequate and dangerous.

Conservative Christianity does not have a monopoly on sentimentality. There are myriad forms of it out there. For the past few months, I have followed in my local newspaper the saga of a stranded orca in the Puget Sound, complete with tales of how the orphaned creature has adopted a pet log as a friend and companion. Yesterday's paper recounted the orca's safe capture, in preparation for an attempt to reunite it with its pod. The other front-page story was that of the Washington Supreme Court ruling that a set of human embryos caught in a custody battle may be destroyed. Today the orca is back on the front page; the embryos are not.

There are times when criticizing sentimentality seems like overkill. But it would be wrong simply to dismiss the phenomenon—and the specific instance I've been discussing, religious kitsch—as nothing more than examples of harmless mediocrity. The great theologian, Cardinal Henri de Lubac, once wrote: "There is nothing more demanding than the taste for mediocrity. Beneath its ever moderate appearance there is nothing more intemperate; nothing surer in its instinct; nothing more pitiless in its refusals. It suffers no greatness, shows beauty no mercy."

Perhaps, at its best, sentimentality strives for something approximating the theological virtues of hope and love. But in refusing to see the world as it is, sentimentality reduces hope to nostalgia. And in seeking to escape ambiguity and the consequences of the Fall, it denies the heart of love, which is compassion. Unless compassion means the act of suffering with the other *in their otherness,* it becomes meaningless. Well-intentioned as the purveyors and consumers of sentiment may be, they still want the luxury of an emotion without having to pay the price for it.

Authorized Versions

AT the height of the recent sexual abuse scandals in the Catholic Church, a writer friend of mine told me that the whole sorry situation had her in a "white rage." I knew exactly what she meant: like most people who have lived through these interminable revelations, I have found myself speechless with fury against those who would wantonly destroy innocence and trust.

But rage is an unwieldy thing. The public reaction to the scandals has unleashed not only informed debate and righteous indignation, but also torrents of verbal abuse and even outright bigotry. A number of prominent writers and artists have piled in, and not just those who have made a living attacking the church. The distinguished Australian novelist, Thomas Keneally, wrote a long essay in the *New Yorker* about his traumatic departure from Catholic seminary on the eve of his ordination. His conclusion: that the church is "a cold and largely self-interested corporate institution."

This is where we need to exercise caution. Keneally's use of the corporate metaphor is typical of contemporary confusion over the difference between authority and power. For many people, there is essentially no distinction between the two words. The Catholic Church's teaching authority, for example, is seen as a quantum of power held by a few shadowy figures in the Vatican. Of course, the same argument is routinely applied to institutional religion of any sort.

But this is to misperceive the nature of authority, and to reduce it to mere fiat, a simple deprivation of freedom. According to sociologist Robert Nisbet, the conflict is not between authority and freedom. "Apart from authority," he once wrote, "there can be no freedom, no individuality." The rise of centralized power —both in church and state—is the result of a *crisis* in authority. Nisbet writes: "We are prone to see the advance of power in the modern world as a consequence...of the diminution of individual freedom. But a more useful way would be to see it in terms of the retreat of authority in many of the areas of society within which human beings commonly find roots and a sense of the larger whole."

Authority as a place of communal shelter and grounding? It is difficult for Americans, schooled as we are in the tradition of individualism, to think in such terms. But as many social theorists have pointed out, individualism reduces us to social atoms, making us more prey to power. Power is based on external constraint whereas authority is based on consent.

In theological terms, true authority is not force, but persuasion; the truest response to authority is not fear but awe. "And they were astonished at his doctrine: for he taught them as one that had authority, and not as the scribes." For a Christian, the authority of Christ is derived not just from his divinity, but from his compelling teaching and witness; the two things are inseparable.

The root of the word means "to nurture something in its growth, to bring increase." Jesus makes it clear that the nature of his authority is not to rule, but to serve. The central paradox of faith is that authority involves *kenosis,* self-emptying.

Of course, as theologian Hans Urs von Balthasar puts it: "In Christ, nature and behavior coincide." In human beings the relationship between imitating the divine nature and day-to-day behavior is much more tenuous. And there's the rub. If the proper emotion before authority is awe, it is easy for that openness and trust to be abused. Some of the best writers and filmmakers have produced chilling tales of that sort of abuse.

That such horror stories should be told unflinchingly is beyond question. One of the real advantages to modern individualism is that our skeptical, psychologically informed sensibilities are more alert to those who use their religious office, and the awe that surrounds it, for their own ends—those, in short, who have sacrificed authority for power.

But here is a question that isn't asked often enough these days: Which artists and writers today are conveying a vision of true spiritual authority? The ancient aesthetic conundrum—why is evil so much easier to depict, and so much more convincing, than good?—applies here, too. How common to see tales of corrupt authority, how rare to experience the elusive, emotional tug of true authority.

It can be done. In the twentieth century, a surprising number of

novels and stories explored the paradox of fallible human beings
attempting to mediate divine authority: Georges Bernanos's
tubercular country cleric, Graham Greene's "whisky priest," Walker
Percy's Father Smith in his fire tower, and Frederick Buechner's
tragicomic figures of Bebb and Godric, to name just a few.

Then there's the gruff priest in Flannery O'Connor's story, "The
Enduring Chill." The protagonist, Asbury, is an alienated intellectual
and hypochondriac who summons a Catholic priest to his sickbed in
a fit of postmodern playfulness.

> "I wonder what you think of Joyce, Father?"
> The priest lifted his chair and pushed closer. "You'll have to
> shout," he said. "Blind in one eye and deaf in one ear."
> "What do you think of Joyce?" Asbury said louder.
> "Joyce? Joyce who?" asked the priest.
> "James Joyce," Asbury said and laughed.
> The priest brushed his huge hand in the air as if he were
> bothered by gnats. "I haven't met him," he said. "Now. Do you say
> your morning and night prayers?"

Blind in one eye and deaf in one ear: are these defects merely
symbolic of the flaws we inevitably find in our ministers? Perhaps.
But perhaps O'Connor is also suggesting that the loss of these
worldly senses may be balanced by an inner eye and ear attuned to
otherworldly stimuli. What these fictional clerics share in common
is that by the end of their stories they speak with the voice of
authority to the extent that they have become true servants.
O'Connor's busy, ill-educated priest comes out to a remote country
house to respond to what is, in essence, a prank call. Irritating as he
might feel the situation to be, he sticks to his basic duty: challenging

Asbury, in true apostolic fashion, to move beyond intellectual posturing to making an act of faith in something beyond himself.

The selfless heroism the characters in these stories achieve comes not in spite of their brokenness, but in and through it. Mysteriously, they become more than they are: they take on the image of the one they have faithfully followed.

If there is an imaginative challenge for our time, it is to hear and transmit the still small voice of divine authority amid the cacophony of individualism and power politics, and to show that the astonishment we feel in the presence of that voice will lead not toward oppression, but toward true community.

Mending the Broken Estate

JAMES Wood is a literary critic to die for. Earnest, passionate, and erudite, Wood's lucid, distinctive voice has cut a wide swathe through what often seem like the mutterings and tergiversations of contemporary literary discourse. Still in his thirties, this British expatriate is now the in-house critic at *The New Republic* and his first collection of essays, *The Broken Estate*, was published with the cultural imprimatur of The Modern Library.

Part of Wood's appeal is that he blends the business of literary interpretation with the muscular assertions of a moralist—a rare combination these days. Less than a month after the events of 9/11, Wood wrote a short, scathing denunciation of contemporary American fiction, deriding the two dominant schools of writing—the postmodern zaniness of "hysterical realism," with its weakness for pop culture and irony, and the misguided attempt to write the Great American Social Novel. "Both genres look a little busted," he wrote.

"That may allow a space for the aesthetic, for the contemplative, for novels that tell us not 'how the world works' but 'how somebody felt about something.'" Of course, Wood's moralism has earned him plenty of enemies. One critic claims that "in the garden of modern letters," Wood "wields a chain saw," and that "he sees books to be reviewed as waiting to be put out of their misery."

But in *The Broken Estate* Wood goes beyond morality to invoke larger metaphysical justifications for his critical enterprise. In the final essay of the collection, Wood offers autobiographical clues about the sources of his convictions. He recounts a youth immersed in Christianity, in both the evangelical world of his family and the more liturgical form he encountered as a chorister at Durham Cathedral. Though he claims his was a happy childhood, not all was well with the young Wood. The overbearing evangelicalism of his parents "excited in me two childish responses: fear and slyness." By the age of fifteen, he felt the need to tear himself away from belief in God.

Left to itself, Wood's account of his loss of faith is poignant but hardly original. It is in the introduction to *The Broken Estate* that Wood lays down a more provocative intellectual challenge. Explaining the title of the book, he argues that the "old estate," which encompassed Western history from the advent of Christianity to the nineteenth century—differentiated the truth-claims of the Bible from those of fiction. The emergence of the realistic novel in the 1800s, Wood claims, did as much as Marx and Darwin to subvert the authority of religion. "At the high point of the novel's triumph, the Gospels began to be read, by both writers and theologians, as a set of fictional tales—as a kind of novel. Simultaneously, fiction became an almost religious activity."

Wood sees the break with the old estate as a terrible cultural impoverishment. Religion becomes either "comforting poetry" or "empty moralism" while fiction, burdened by the need to supplant religion, falls into aestheticism.

It is a compelling insight. But the irony here is that Wood, who in one of the essays in this collection castigates T.S. Eliot as an anti-Semite and religious fundamentalist, bases his book on a supremely Eliotic point, a reworded version of the poet's famous "dissociation of sensibility" argument.

Moreover, it isn't clear whether Wood really believes that the broken estate should be mended. The glory of fiction, he writes, is that it doesn't compel belief. Because its depiction of reality is always bracketed by the "as if" and "not quite," fiction merely requests our belief. In the end, the reality portrayed in fiction can only be validated by its readers: "fiction is proved by what it discloses, and is thus always a running test case of itself."

Over against fiction Wood places religion, which stands or falls on its truth claims. "Once religion is revealed to you, you are never free." But instead of attacking believers outright, Wood pays a sort of backhanded tribute to those who accept the "logical claustrophobia" of Christianity.

Wood seems to content himself with the twofold task of celebrating the great writers who "move between the religious impulse and the novelistic impulse" and "draw on both," such as Melville, Flaubert, Joyce, and Woolf, and denouncing those writers who fail to do so.

Such a critical program is noble in its way—his essays are filled with brilliant readings and epigrammatic wisdom—but it seems oddly lacking in ambition after Wood has raised so many urgent cosmological issues. One reason for this loss of nerve may be that his distinction between fiction and religion is muddled. In his book *A Palpable God* the novelist Reynolds Price agrees with Wood that fiction requests a suspension of our disbelief. Price goes on to note that scripture, by contrast, simply tells the story, leaving it for us to believe or not.

By always speaking of religion rather than faith, Wood's diction plays on the modern suspicion of institutional religion, which sees belief in terms of coercion and enslavement. But for many of us faith is also "proved by what it discloses." To say this is not to collapse faith and fiction into a single category, but to say that they are analogous. The difference lies in what they ask us to believe. Faith, which always comes accompanied by doubt, embodies the freedom of trust. But faith remains—or should remain—a "test case" throughout one's life.

For a growing number of writers and artists, the need to distinguish between the novelistic impulse and the religious impulse has taken on new meaning. They, too, draw on both, give both their due, and thus mend the broken estate.

My Grandfather's Easel

MY earliest recollection of my grandfather, James Nicol, comes from a trip to Britain when I was very small. Seeing him and my grandmother was a special treat, because we lived in New York and they lived far away in a place called South Africa. On this trip, however, we were all visiting their native Scotland. Sitting in a hotel dining room, surrounded by what seemed like acres of white linen tablecloths and armories full of silver cutlery, my grandfather taught me European table manners (fork upside down).

That I remember him in this way seems right, for he always represented to me the epitome of what a gentleman should be. For a long time, the word gentleman also had a literal connotation for me, because James Nicol was, in fact, a gentle man: quiet but sociable, kind and observant, never the center of attention but always a lively presence. And he had style. He was a natty, if not flashy, dresser—his hats smart, his ties crisply knotted. I was not surprised to learn that in the war he had known and worked with Sean Connery. I could imagine the two of them over drinks and cigarettes, their underlying Scots toughness somehow making them more rather than less sophisticated than their effete English counterparts.

Like so many Scots down the centuries, he emigrated in search of adventure and better opportunities. He certainly found both in Johannesburg, becoming the art director and partner of an advertising agency. He did well enough to retire early and pursue his dream of painting full time.

That's how I knew him, as someone who worked behind an easel. Certain things about his painting became clear to me, even at an early age. He loved landscapes, still lifes, and nudes. Though he lived halfway across the world, his paintings hung on our walls.

Portraits were something more fraught for him. It was clear to me that he was daunted by the challenge of getting a likeness, not because he was timid but because his standards were high. And yet he wanted so very much to paint his grandchildren. I have his unfinished portrait of my sister, done when she was about six. I also watched him paint it, transfixed by the way his pale blue eyes would dart back and forth between Kathryn and the canvas. The intensity of his concentration stirred within me something close to awe. He abandoned the painting, as he did a number of portraits. Gazing at it today—even in its unfinished state—I see my sister's heart and soul. No painting of me, if one was ever undertaken, survives.

As I grew older, I began to realize that my grandfather painted in oil in the style of Impressionism. He loved Renoir and Monet, to be sure, but he also championed some of the lesser-known Impressionists, including Sisley and Caillebotte, artists whose work I had to unearth in libraries.

At some point I began to question—perhaps even to become critical of—his working in what I thought of as an outmoded style. But then he would do something that would catch me off guard. When I was ten, for example, he spent nine months living in Florence in order to study under the disciples of the great Annigoni. He would have been about sixty at the time. They told him he needed to work in egg tempera, a medium he had to learn from scratch.

Then, in his late seventies and eighties, his palette underwent a remarkable change. He reenacted the movement from Impressionism to Post-Impressionism. Suddenly his colors lightened, moving increasingly toward the purples, pinks, and light greens of late Monet and the favorite of his old age, Pierre Bonnard. He began to experiment with paintings dominated by a single color—using only shades of red or of green to render an entire still life. One day, visiting him in Massachusetts, where he and my grandmother had moved to be near my mother, I looked at the easel, only to see a canvas in the style of Henri Matisse, with simplified planes of bolder primary colors. The old sense of awe returned.

Since he didn't exhibit his work much in his later years, I don't know how many people knew what was happening on his easel. I tried to express my admiration to him, but always felt awkward and shy about it. In turn, he had a reticence about discussing *Image* with me. But our love and our pride in one another leapt over the gaps in our conversation.

There came a time when he could no longer hold a paintbrush and eventually a time when he had to go to a nursing home. When I visited him there, I felt stifled by the institutional blandness of his room, and mourned the lack of beauty around him. My family understandably was far too preoccupied simply meeting his daily needs to give much thought to matters of aesthetics, but on that trip I managed to get to a print shop in Boston. They had one print left by Pierre Bonnard, *The Open Window*. It shows a domestic interior with a woman asleep in a chair and an impish black cat in the lower right corner. But the painting is really of the window and what lies beyond it. The reds, oranges, and blues of the interior are bisected by a large vertical shutter in white. The glory of the painting, however, is the shimmering foliage of the trees outside the window, a canopy of green against a pale blue sky. My grandfather was not someone who spoke publicly or confidently about religion, but in some profound way I think that the Bonnard painting served as an icon for him—something for him to gaze upon, in his last days, with those pale blue eyes.

Shaggy Dog Stories

BACK when this journal was nothing more than a mere
proposal, I sought out a meeting with the distinguished church
historian Martin Marty to enlist his support. Despite his frenetic
schedule, he responded immediately, offering to meet me for a drink
when next I came to Chicago. When we got together the conversation
eventually turned to some of the writers who would become guiding
spirits for this journal. We spoke of such twentieth-century figures as
T.S. Eliot, Georges Bernanos, Graham Greene, Flannery O'Connor, and
Walker Percy, who had re-imagined the Christian faith for a secular
age. Marty pondered that list for a moment. "It's fascinating," he said,
"that nearly all of these figures, who could write in such a sophisticated
way about the complexities and ambiguities of modern life, held such
conservative theological views. I'm not sure I can account for that.
Someone ought to study the phenomenon."

That comment has often come back to me, since it touches on a fundamental paradox. Why has the lion's share of art inspired by religious faith grown out of an engagement with religious orthodoxy— with the ancient dogmas of the faith in their full-blooded form? One

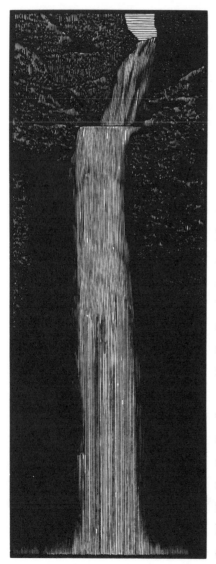

author on the list might be considered an exception to the argument: Graham Greene, who can hardly be held up as a champion of orthodoxy. For much of his life he was an acerbic critic of church authority. But the novels of his that seem likely to stand the test of time are *The Power and the Glory, The End of the Affair,* and *The Heart of the Matter*—all written soon after his conversion to Catholicism and steeped in the central mysteries of the church.

The truth is that whatever wisdom and compassion the great Jewish and Christian artists manifest come not because they skirt around orthodoxy, but because they have entered into its depths and come out transformed. The word dogma has few positive connotations for modern ears. In her book *Amazing Grace: A Vocabulary of Faith,* Kathleen Norris takes on dogma as one of the words that she and millions of others find off-putting about the Christian faith. She points out that its original Greek root means "what seems good, fitting, becoming" and relates that to the process of consensus in the church, the evolution of the church's understanding of the truths of revelation. Seizing on the words "good, fitting, becoming," Norris goes on to say that "the word 'beauty' might be a more fitting synonym for dogma than what has become its synonym in contemporary English: 'doctrine,' or a teaching."

With her analogy to beauty, Norris has intuited something profound about dogma, but she doesn't go far enough. The central dogmas of the Judeo-Christian tradition derive not from a priori theological statements, but directly from the Bible, which is predominantly a narrative, and not a work of theology. For Jews the story centers on a covenant. For Christians, the narrative continues, and is recounted in the church's creeds. And what is a creed but a story—a cosmic story, to be sure—that moves from the Father who created heaven and earth, to the advent of the Son, whose life, death and resurrection redeemed fallen mankind, to the presence among us of the Holy Spirit, who is made known in the church, sacraments, and our fellow believers?

The poet W.H. Auden, another Christian writer, said that "Dogmatic theological statements are neither logical propositions nor poetic utterances. They are 'shaggy dog' stories; they have a point, but he who tries too hard to get it will miss it." Individual doctrines are short stories from a collection of interconnected tales. You can tell them out of order, but you can't violate what screenwriters call the arc of the larger story.

In short, dogmas are not dry bits of theological rationalism, but deeply metaphorical attempts to enshrine mystery. To vary the analogy, dogma are not so much efforts to give logical accounts of the mysteries of revelation as they are a process of creating a tabernacle for the shining mysteries within.

The tabernacle exists to protect the mystery from vandalism of various kinds, from efforts to reduce it to brittle abstraction or comfortable illusion. It is well known that the church has tended to define dogma only in reaction to the rise of particular heresies. Of course, the word heresy itself comes with its own set of oversized baggage these days. Too often we think of heresy only in terms of lurid Hollywood tableaux, complete with angry, repressed inquisitors, terrified victims, and blazing bonfires. But that is to give in to a classic stereotype of the church as mere center of power and the heretic as gallant rebel. The church's struggle with heresy has been, by and large, not so much an attempt to repress dissent as a call to the entire church to embrace the mysteries in all their richness. One of the oldest definitions of heresy, in fact, is simply imbalance, a stressing of one term in a divine paradox over another, as in the early christological heresies that elevated Christ's divinity over his humanity, or vice versa. G.K. Chesterton had it right: "The whole secret of mysticism is this: that a man can understand everything by the help of what he does not understand. The morbid logician seeks to make everything lucid, and succeeds in making everything mysterious. The mystic allows one thing to be mysterious, and everything else becomes lucid ... [The Christian] puts the seed of dogma in a central darkness; but it branches forth in all directions with abounding natural health ...."

Acknowledgments

THIS book is not merely a collection of essays, but in a certain sense the chronicle of a journal. As in the movie industry, the production of a literary and arts journal is a large, collaborative activity. Indeed, over the span of years, the enterprise comes to resemble a Cecil B. DeMille epic. So it would truly be no exaggeration to say that I ought to thank "a cast of thousands," from friends and family to literary and artistic contributors to financial donors and institutional hosts.

In short, the task is impossible. But at the risk of leaving too many people out I will mention a few.

I would like to thank, first and foremost, my wife Suzanne, whose imprint is not only over every page of this book, but on the vision that lies behind *Image* itself. She and my four children—Magdalen, Helena, Charles, and Benedict—have made huge personal sacrifices for the sake of *Image,* far beyond what is fair or reasonable. By the grace of their love, *Image* exists.

At the very beginning were Maclin and Karen Horton, along with the journal's co-founders, Harold Fickett and Luci Shaw. Three enormously gifted managing editors—Richard Wilkinson, Bill Coleman, and Mary Kenagy—have labored mightily to keep *Image* alive and well and have left their own distinctive marks on its pages. An army of bright, energetic student interns have served the journal and its other programs.

Thanks to my board of directors, especially the chair, Carol Windham, and Jane Owen, who have been such stalwart friends. I'm also grateful to my colleagues and students at Seattle Pacific University for providing such a strong foundation for our daily work.

Barry Moser and Alfonse Borysewicz, two distinguished artists, have generously given some of their work to help this book better incarnate its theme. At Square Halo Books, Ned Bustard has been both an irrepressible encourager and a talented designer.

Finally, a bow to all who have read and responded so powerfully and movingly to *Image* over the years. You have helped to forge a community that has done much to redeem the time.

A Note About the Artists Featured in the Book

ALFONSE BORYSEWICZ, whose painting *Strata XXX, Ash Wednesday* is featured on the front cover of this book, was awarded Pollack-Krasner Grants in 1987 and 1992, and received a Guggenheim Fellowship in Painting in 1995. His work appears in numerous private and public collections, including those of Microsoft and General Electric, and was featured in *Image* #32. His last exhibit, *Letters,* was exhibited at the Cathedral of St. John the Divine in New York and Francine Seders Gallery in Seattle.

BARRY MOSER, whose illustrations appear throughout this book, is widely considered one of America's leading artists and illustrators. He was educated at Auburn University, the University of Chattanooga, and the University of Massachusetts, Amherst. He is a member of the National Academy of Design and has served on the faculty of Rhode Island School of Design. His work can be found in numerous collections and libraries around the world, including the National Gallery of Art in Washington, D.C., the Metropolitan Museum, the British Museum, the Library of Congress, the New York Public Library, the National Library of Australia, the Vatican Library, the Victoria and Albert Museum, and the Israel Museum in Jerusalem. As illustrator, author, and designer, Moser has produced over two hundred and fifty titles, including the Arion Press *Moby-Dick* and the University of California Press edition of *The Divine Comedy,* translated by Allen Mandelbaum. His 1999 edition of the King James Bible has received international acclaim and was the subject of an award-winning documentary film called *A Thief Among the Angels.*

About the Author

GREGORY WOLFE is the publisher and editor of *Image: A Journal of the Arts and Religion* and the Director of the Center for Religious Humanism. He also serves as Writer in Residence at Seattle Pacific University.

Among his books are *Malcolm Muggeridge: A Biography* (ISI Books) and *Sacred Passion: The Art of William Schickel* (University of Notre Dame Press).

Wolfe is also the editor of *The New Religious Humanists: A Reader* (Free Press) and the co-author of *Circle of Grace: Praying with—and for—Your Children* (Ballantine Books), *Books That Build Character* (Touchstone), *Climb High, Climb Far* (Fireside), and *The Family New Media Guide* (Touchstone).

He has published essays, reviews, and articles in numerous journals, including *Commonweal, First Things, National Review, Crisis, Modern Age,* and *New Oxford Review.* He received his B.A., summa cum laude, from Hillsdale College and his M.A. in English literature from Oxford University.